The Rhetoric of Diversity and the Traditions of American Literary Study

Critical Studies in Education and Culture Series

Adult Students "At Risk": Culture Bias in Higher Education
Timothy William Quinnan

Education and the Postmodern Condition
Michael Peters, editor

Restructuring for Integrative Education: Multiple Perspectives, Multiple Contexts
Todd E. Jennings, editor

Postmodern Philosophical Critique and the Pursuit of Knowledge in Higher Education
Roger P. Mourad, Jr.

Naming the Multiple: Poststructuralism and Education
Michael Peters, editor

Literacy in the Library: Negotiating the Spaces Between Order and Desire
Mark Dressman

Thinking Again: Education After Postmodernism
Nigel Blake, Paul Smeyers, Richard Smith, and Paul Standish

Racial Categorization of Multiracial Children in Schools
Jane Ayers Chiong

bell hooks' Engaged Pedagogy: Education for Critical Consciousness
Namulundah Florence

Wittgenstein: Philosophy, Postmodernism, Pedagogy
Michael Peters and James Marshall

Policy, Pedagogy, and Social Inequality: Community College Student Realities in Post-Industrial America
Penelope E. Herideen

Psychoanalysis and Pedagogy
Stephen Appel, editor

The Rhetoric of Diversity and the Traditions of American Literary Study

Critical Multiculturalism in English

LESLIEE ANTONETTE

Critical Studies in Education and Culture Series
Edited by Henry A. Giroux

BERGIN & GARVEY
Westport, Connecticut · London

Library of Congress Cataloging-in-Publication Data

Antonette, Lesliee, 1958–
 The rhetoric of diversity and the traditions of American literary study : critical multiculturalism in English / Lesliee Antonette.
   p.   cm.—(Critical studies in education and culture series, ISSN 1064-8615)
 Includes bibliographical references and index.
 ISBN 0-89789-546-0 (alk. paper)
 1. American literature—History and criticism—Theory, etc. 2. Rhetoric—Social aspects—United States—History. 3. Literature and society—United States—History. 4. Pluralism (Social sciences) in literature. 5. English language—United States—Rhetoric. 6. Criticism—United States—History. 7. Multiculturalism—United States. 8. Ethnic groups in literature. I. Title. II. Series.
 PS25.A58   1998
 810.9—dc21   98-9531

British Library Cataloguing in Publication Data is available.

Copyright © 1998 by Lesliee Antonette

All rights reserved. No portion of this book may be reproduced, by any process or technique, without the express written consent of the publisher.

Library of Congress Catalog Card Number: 98-9531

ISBN: 0-89789-546-0
ISSN: 1064-8615

First published in 1998

Bergin & Garvey, 88 Post Road West, Westport, CT 06881
An imprint of Greenwood Publishing Group, Inc.

Printed in the United States of America

The paper used in this book complies with the
Permanent Paper Standard issued by the National
Information Standards Organization (Z39.48–1984).

10 9 8 7 6 5 4 3 2 1

Copyright Acknowledgments

The author and publisher gratefully acknowledge permission to use excerpts from the following.

hooks, bell. "Representations of Whiteness in the Black Imagination." *Black Looks: Race and Representation*. South End Press, 1992. With permission from the publisher, South End Press, 116 Saint Botolph Street, Boston, MA 02155.

For Jeremy Daniel

Contents

Series Foreword *by Henry A. Giroux*	ix
Acknowledgments	xiii
Introduction	1
1. Ethico-Political History and the Production of a Noncritical Multiculturalism	13
2. Reconstructing Multiculturalism Critically	39
3. Critical Multicultural Readings of Four American Texts	67
4. Critical Multicultural Pedagogy	93
Appendix: Multicultural Reading Paradigm	119
Bibliography	129
Index	137

Series Foreword

Educational reform has fallen upon hard times. The traditional assumption that schooling is fundamentally tied to the imperatives of citizenship designed to educate students to exercise civic leadership and public service has been eroded. The schools are now the key institution for producing professional, technically trained, credentialed workers for whom the demands of citizenship are subordinated to the vicissitudes of the marketplace and the commercial public sphere. Given the current corporate and right wing assault on public and higher education, coupled with the emergence of a moral and political climate that has shifted to a new Social Darwinism, the issues that framed the democratic meaning, purpose, and use to which education might aspire have been displaced by more vocational and narrowly ideological considerations.

The war waged against the possibilities of an education wedded to the precepts of a real democracy is not merely ideological. Against the backdrop of reduced funding for public schooling, the call for privatization, vouchers, cultural uniformity, and choice, there are the often ignored larger social realities of material power and oppression. On the national level, there has been a vast resurgence of racism. This is evident in the passing of anti-immigration laws such as Proposition 187 in California, the dismantling of the welfare state, the demonization of black youth that is taking place in the popular media, and the remarkable attention provided by the media to forms of race talk that argue for the intellectual inferiority of blacks or dismiss calls for racial justice as simply a holdover from the "morally bankrupt" legacy of the 1960s.

Poverty is on the rise among children in the United States, with 20 percent of all children under the age of eighteen living below the poverty line. Unemployment is growing at an alarming rate for poor youth of color, especially in the urban centers. While black youth are policed and disciplined in and out of the nation's schools, conservative and liberal educators define education through the ethically limp discourses of privatization, national standards, and global competitiveness.

Many writers in the critical education tradition have attempted to challenge the right wing fundamentalism behind educational and social reform in both the United States and abroad while simultaneously providing- ethical signposts for a public discourse about education and democracy that is both prophetic and transformative. Eschewing traditional categories, a diverse number of critical theorists and educators have successfully exposed the political and ethical implications of the cynicism and despair that has become endemic to the discourse of schooling and civic life. In its place, such educators strive to provide a language of hope that inextricably links the struggle over schooling to understanding and transforming our present social and cultural dangers.

At the risk of overgeneralizing both cultural studies theorists and critical educators have emphasized the importance of understanding theory as the grounded basis for "intervening into contexts and power . . . in order to enable people to act more strategically in ways that may change their context for the better."[1] Moreover, theorists in both fields have argued for the primacy of the political by calling for and struggling to produce critical public spaces, regardless of how fleeting they may be, in which "popular cultural resistance is explored as a form of political resistance."[2] Such writers have analyzed the challenges that teachers will have to face in redefining a new mission for education, one that is linked to honoring the experiences, concerns, and diverse histories and languages that give expression to the multiple narratives that engage and challenge the legacy of democracy

Equally significant is the insight of recent critical educational work that connects the politics of difference with concrete strategies for addressing the crucial relationships between schooling and the economy, and citizenship and the politics of meaning in communities of multicultural, multiracial, and multilingual schools.

Critical Studies in Education and Culture attempts to address and demonstrate how scholars working in the fields of cultural studies and the critical pedagogy might join together in a radical project and practice informed by theoretically rigorous discourses that affirm the critical but refuse the cynical, and establish hope as central to a critical pedagogical and political practice but eschew a romantic utopianism. Central to such a project is the issue of how pedagogy might provide cultural studies theorists and educators with an opportunity to engage pedagogical practices that are not only transdisciplinary, transgressive, and oppositional, but also connected to a wider project designed to further racial, economic, and political democracy.[3] By taking seriously the relations between culture and power, we further the possibilities of resistance, struggle, and change.

Critical Studies in Education and Culture is committed to publishing, work that opens a narrative space that affirms the contextual and the specific while simultaneously recognizing the ways in which such spaces are shot through with issues of power. The series attempts to continue an important legacy of theoretical work in cultural studies in which related debates on pedagogy are understood and addressed within the larger context of social responsibility, civic courage, and the reconstruction of democratic public life. We must keep in mind Raymond Williams's insight that the "deepest impulse (informing cultural politics) is the desire to make learning part of the process of social change itself."[4] Education as a cultural pedagogical practice takes place across multiple sites, which include not only schools and universities but also the mass media, popular culture, and other public spheres, and signals how within diverse contexts, education makes us both subjects of and subject to relations of power.

This series challenges the current return to the primacy of market values and simultaneous retreat from politics so evident in the recent work of educational theorists, legislators, and policy analysts. Professional relegitimation in a troubled time seems to be the order of the day as an increasing number of academics both refuse to recognize public and higher education as critical public spheres and offer little or no resistance to the ongoing vocationalization of schooling, the continuing evisceration of the intellectual labor force and the current assaults on the working poor, the elderly, and women and children.[5]

Emphasizing the centrality of politics, culture, and power, *Critical Studies in Education and Culture* will deal with pedagogical issues that contribute in imaginative and transformative ways to our understanding of how critical knowledge, democratic values, and social practices can provide a basis for teachers, students, and other cultural workers to redefine their role as engaged and public intellectuals. Each volume will attempt to rethink the relationship between language and experience, pedagogy and human agency, and ethics and social responsibility as part of a larger project for engaging and deepening the prospects of democratic schooling in a multiracial and multicultural society. *Critical Studies in Education and Culture* takes on the responsibility of witnessing and addressing the most pressing problems of public schooling and civic life, and engages culture as a crucial site and strategic force for productive social change.

Henry A. Giroux

NOTES

1. Lawrence Grossberg, "Toward a Genealogy of the State of Cultural Studies," in Cary Nelson and Dilip Parameshwar Gaonkar, eds. *Disciplinarity and Dissent in Cultural Studies* (New York: Routledge, 1996), 143.

2. David Bailey and Stuart Hall, "The Vertigo of Displacement," *Ten 8* 2:3 (1992), 19.

3. My notion of transdisciplinary comes from Mas'ud Zavarzadeh and Donald Morton, "Theory, Pedagogy, Politics: The Crisis of the 'Subject' in the Humanities," in *Theory Pedagogy Politics: Texts for Change,* Mas'ud Zavarzadeh and Donald Morton, eds. (Urbana: University of Illinois Press, 1992), 10. At issue here is neither ignoring the boundaries of discipline-based knowledge nor simply fusing different disciplines, but creating theoretical paradigms, questions, and knowledge that cannot be taken up within the policed boundaries of the existing disciplines.

4. Raymond Williams, "Adult Education and Social Change," in *What I Came to Say* (London: Hutchinson-Radus, 1989), 158

5. The term "professional legitimation" comes from a personal correspondence with Professor Jeff Williams of East Carolina University.

Acknowledgments

I would like to acknowledge Professor Henry Giroux for allowing me the opportunity to consider the concept of critical multiculturalism within the framework of critical education. It is through the work of Professor Giroux and the work he has sponsored that I have gained access to critical theories of education. His work has been a significant influence on my work. I would also like to thank him for this opportunity to enter into the professional conversation regarding critical multiculturalism. I am also directly indebted to the work of Paolo Friere. Through the work of Professor Giroux, and also through the work of Ira Shor, I was allowed to see a model of what I thought education should be. Giroux helped me translate the theory at work in Friere's work, and Shor provided me with a practical model. In my own work, I have to put them together. Not that the work of either Giroux or Shor suffers in theory and practice, but that is how I was able to synthesize Friere.

In my understanding of Friere there is a bottom line and that is that in an educational process there is no bottom line. Learning is a fluid, individual, constant process. When students become aware of their ability to learn in myriad situations and learn that they control the process, they become invested members of the knowledge-making community. In American culture this is necessarily a multicultural endeavor. The multicultural reality of the United States of America is not something that must be accommodated; it is a source of great wisdom and knowledge. It is a reality that we need to engage and investigate. It is a reality that we need to "see" at work in our everyday lives. Critical pedagogy, critical literacy, liberatory education, citizenship education, and critical multiculturalism are all attempts at gaining access to that reality and the meaning it offers us as a culture. These are very different projects than the "celebration" of difference and diversity, a noncritical pedagogy, theory and multiculturalism offer. A critical multiculturalism attempts to make visible the means through which multicultural reality has been subordinated to a monocultural hegemonic agenda. The argument that this work finally rests upon is this: a critical multiculturalism may produce a multicultural hegemonic agenda that cannot replicate the problems and issues that concern a monocultural hegemonic agenda. This, however, does not mean that a critical multicultural hegemonic agenda will not possess its own set of problems and issues.

I am indebted to Professor Steven Gould Axelrod for my participation in this conversation. His patience, wisdom, and encouragement have kept me at work. Thank you for being so generous with your time. I needed quite a bit of it to think through this maze of multiculturalism. Professor Axelrod allowed me to follow my interest in a topic that was new, uncertain, and confusing. However, I needed to know more about it, and he respected my need to know. He not only supported my interest; he challenged it. He made me articulate the value I saw in entering this conversation. This taught me that I could control my educational experience, and reinforced the idea that my interests are valid and useful. The educational experience provided by Professor Axelrod informed my own teaching style. He was encouraging, supportive, and firm in his refusal to accept anything less than the best I could produce. When I said that it was the best I could do, he believed me and then showed me how to improve it.

I would also like to thank Professor Rise B. Axelrod for her kindness, patience, and direction. I had the opportunity to study with Professor Axelrod at California State University at San Bernardino. She was a rigorous and exciting teacher, and she has become a supportive friend and a role model for me.

This work has been influenced by the presence of some truly great professors at the University of California at Riverside. Emory Elliott, Joe Childers, Richard Boyd, George Haggerty, Carole Fabricant, Traise Yamamoto, and Gregory Bredbeck have all contributed to my ability to produce this project. This work comes directly from my own student experience. As a nontraditional re-entry student and single parent, I came to the university to learn about the world, and these professors taught me. Aside from the many valuable academic skills I learned from these professors, I also learned some poignant life lessons. That is the mark of a quality education. The one skill that all of these professors taught me in one form or another, and for which I am eternally grateful, is silence. The absence of verbal expression does not equal the absence of power. Power exists in myriad forms and relationships. Sometimes silence can be the most powerful position one can occupy. All of these professors taught me how to pick my battles and how to use my silence, as well as my words, to my greatest advantage. I hope I have produced a text that illustrates the quality of the education I have received.

Without the help of my great friend, Lois Stephenson, this book would have been much harder to produce. Her emotional and technical support is invaluable. She is the best friend a writer could hope for. Her knowledge and experience in the field of writing are vast and she shared it all with me. Lois has been a haven for me. She has protected me, fed me, encouraged me, corrected me, and helped me to become a stronger human being and a much better writer.

I would like to thank Kate Watt for her unerring sense of what to ask next. Kate's questioning of my argument helped to shape it in its early form and helped me to refine it later in the process of writing. I want to thank Sean Connelly, Josh Stein, and Darnetta Elaine Bell, Ph.Diva for their friendship and support. They know my argument just about as well as I do. I am grateful to Andre Salazar for feeding me, and to Andre and Professor Katherine Atkinson Lauricha for letting me whine. I want to extend thanks to Harry Walsh; his absence from the academy is a serious loss to the profession. My son, Jeremy, is the reason I do anything. Without him this book would not exist. Thanks for being here. I owe a special thanks to my own Steven Verwey.

I am indebted to those I have named. I also want to acknowledge the editorial staff at Greenwood Publishing. They were helpful, supportive, and patient with me as I learned how to produce a published text. I am also grateful to East Stroudsburg University for providing me with the material to make the ideas in this book reality. I hope that the positive parts of this text will be viewed as a reflection of those influences I have named, and that the negative parts will be attributed to my own limitations.

Introduction

I had just finished the first major rewrite of this text and I was hungry. It was the first of the month and I had no food in the house, but I did have money in the bank. As I headed to my neighborhood grocery store, I shuddered at the realization that it was "Mother's day." In my neighborhood Mother's day falls on the first and fifteenth of every month. It is the day welfare checks arrive. I lived near the university where I taught, and the neighborhoods that border the university are made up of low-income families who live in public housing. The grocery store I frequent caters to those in the lower economic echelons. Not coincidentally, it is the best place to stock up on "ethnic food" staples, and on the first and the fifteenth of every month it is full of welfare moms, dads, and kids doing their shopping.

Having been a welfare mom for a significant portion of my adult life (even a small amount of time is significant), I was not uncomfortable in the fray—I was just hungry and did not want to wait in line. I went anyway—it was early, I told myself, maybe I will beat the rush. I did. Much to my pleasure the store was only moderately peopled. I did my shopping and as I was standing in line I allowed my eyes to wander around the store. Something tickled my nose, and when I sneezed the man behind me said "GawBress you." I turned to thank him and thought, "How nice." Mother's day is usually a day fraught with not-so repressed anxiety and tension. I looked behind the man who had responded to my sneeze and noted that the child in his grocery cart had a much darker complexion than the man I had assumed to be his father. I had, by now, identified the man as being Japanese or possibly Japanese American. But, looking at his son, I began to reconsider this judgment. When a woman who appeared to be the boy's mother walked up and began to speak to the Japanese/Japanese American man in a distinctly Hispanic accent, I was surprised. The accent of the woman and the accent of the man were so clearly different that I was at first fascinated by what I perceived to be their bi-cultural union. I began to wonder if I had simply misheard the man's accent, and I found myself watching this family out of the corner of my eye, trying to make sense of the physiological presentation of the family members, and my interest in them.

We made it through the line and the woman paid with food stamps. As I was standing across from the Japanese/American/Mexican man, who had offered me God's blessing, bagging groceries, an older woman with a light complexion and dark hair walked over and asked him, in a very thick German accent, if she might use his cart.

"No." He responded, "Am stir using."
"Oh." She smiled. "I'm sorry."
"That's okay." He smiled back.

I stood watching this exchange, and I thought to myself, this is my world. This is my grocery store, and these are the people I interact with in the course of fulfilling my needs of subsistence. This thought entered my mind and for one-half of a second I was filled with a warm feeling of . . . power. Then the realization struck me that not only had I appropriated the experiences of these people in the grocery store as somehow being "my own," I had distanced myself from my own experience as well. I felt like an anthropologist in the field.

I tried to make some sense out of my realization, as I walked out to the parking lot and looked around for my vehicle. I saw two African American women trying to get their kids into a late sixties Chevy Impala, and a Chicano or Mexican man in a really old Ford pickup trying to get their parking space. A young, Anglo-American man with one arm approached me, while I surveyed the parking lot. He wanted a dollar. As I proceeded to my JEEP, I began to wonder what those around me might be thinking about me. After all, I was walking through the parking lot analyzing those I encountered. I wondered what it was they saw when they looked at me. I suddenly felt really "white." When this thought occurred to me I found that I had a definition of what it meant to be "white" already in my head. To be white in America is to be perceptibly Anglo-American *and* middle class. I wondered if this was the image of me perceived by those people in the store and parking lot; and I wondered how I was supposed to reconcile my feeling of "Americanness" in the parking lot with the feeling of belonging I had inside the grocery store. This lead to some clarity on one problem I had encountered in the process of writing this book. What is multicultural is somehow not fully American. This left me to ponder the connection I felt to these people and this place, and the differences that were jarring me but not readily perceptible.

I had associated an Anglo appearance with being middle-class and those two characteristics were somehow, in my mind equated with being American. If this were so, then based on their appearances the people in the store and the people in the parking lot where somehow not as American as I had felt. These people were for the most part not Anglo and the one clearly Anglo individual did not appear to be middle class. However, I had based all of these assumptions upon the difference between their appearances and mine. I was quite surprised by this realization. After all I was shopping at the same store and buying the same kind of food. I was dressed in a similar fashion. In fact, I believed this in spite of the fact that I am frequently identified by people as a member of one or another ethnic group other than Anglo.

Finally, it occurred to me that the feelings of community I had experienced in the store had begun to shift when I saw the Japanese American man's wife pay for her groceries in food stamps. Physiological appearance had nothing to do with the feelings of difference I had experienced. I had just spent all but ten dollars of my teaching assistant paycheck on groceries, my son's college tuition bill was waiting to be paid when I got home, and I was looking at repaying student loans for the rest of my life. In economic terms I was not very different from the welfare mother I had once been. However, standing in the store and walking through the parking lot I was keenly aware of the differences between my current situation and the situation I was once in as a welfare mother.

I felt superior to my old self and to that family who had paid their grocery bill with food stamps. I felt like the great surveyor. After all, I had just written a book about "these people." That store suddenly felt a million miles away from the university just three blocks away. And yet, I wanted to stay there with those supermarket people because to look at the differences between us meant I had to look at the differences that existed within me. I had to look at the ways in which I had hierarchized those differences as more and less valuable, and I had to look at the ways in which I had translated that hierarchy onto the people who surrounded me in the world primarily, based on their appearances, but also based on their appearances in specific situations.

Everything I had learned in eight years of studying American literature, two years of writing a dissertation on multiculturalism and five years of teaching what I think a critical multicultural pedagogy is was being played out in front of me in living Technicolor. And, I had performed it. This course of study had taught me that Anglo is a nonmarked category of American identity. Those who appear Anglo can assume the attributes of American identity even if lived experience does not meet the criteria. They can disappear into the cloak of Americanness. Those who do not have those physiological attributes remain marked as somehow not fully American. It was the process of differentiation, categorization, and hierarchization that I experienced during my trip to the grocery store that crystallized for me the work I have done in the pages that follow. The phenomenon of difference as exemplified in my store and in myself made clear to me the ways in which my life in American culture has trained me to think about difference. The habit of thinking requires that I read certain physiological markers as universal indicators of characteristics that are immutable. This way of seeing locks individuals into false and invidious positions of difference, for these differences are always hierarchized.

If the man in the store appears to be an immigrant, welfare dad, then by virtue of my more Anglo appearance I exist at a "step up" from him at American and middle class. However, that was not my lived experience. I was living on "Academic welfare." I lived on loan checks and a teaching assistant's stipend. My son attended college on grant money and the little I could contribute. We were the educated poor, but we had potential. In spite of my education and my self-conscious awareness of my differences from both the academic community and the welfare community, I found that the hierarchization of that difference was automatic. I wondered if this process of hierarchizing difference was just my own idiosyncratic way of looking at the world. I think not.

This work illustrates that the logic system within which I am constructed as a meaningful human entity is one that has trained me to think in such hierarchical terms. This realization has serious implications for any consideration of multiculturalism. It is a crucial part of any attempt to move beyond the vast body of work produced in the name of multiculturalism toward a critical consideration of the ways in which that discourse was produced and functions within the institution that produces it. K. Anthony Appiah ends his essay "The Multiculuralist Misunderstanding" by writing, "it is not the black culture the racist disdains, but blacks" (Appiah, 1997: 36). Appiah's argument is that the conflation of racially marked difference with cultural difference is a road well-traveled, but, perhaps, not well-scrutinized by multiculturalism. I cannot agree with Appiah's conclusion that we should let the cultural "field lie fallow." It is a necessary chore to inspect the ways in which this conflation has occurred and the function it serves. As my opening story illustrates, for a majority of Americans everyday reality in America is a multinational, multiethnic, multicultural experience contained within the rubric of American culture. People grocery shop, send their children to college, and buy homes that may never speak fluent English or even vote. They are American. That is the national alliance they have chosen and the culture they practice. To name them multicultural reinforces the same separatist logic that physiological marking serves. It is a separation that mimics the categorization, and hierarchization process that occurs as we look at other people. In other words it continues a separation process that has historically led to racism, sexism, and homophobia.

In this work I distinguish between a critical multiculturalism and a noncritical multiculturalism. Through a consideration of the concept and practices of a noncritical multiculturalism, as it has functioned historically and as it is widely theorized and practiced in American university English programs, I have found that it serves to reproduce privileged discourse that inadvertently, and even in the face of the best intentions, reproduces the same oppressive practices it would resist in the academic communities of composition and literature. The value of such an argument is in mapping how this occurs. Through an application of the tenets of critical theory, per the Frankfurt School, and the works of Paolo Friere, Henry Giroux, Ira Shor, Henry Louis Gates, Jr., Toni Morrison, David Theo Goldberg, Kathleen McCormick, Homi Bhaba, Jurgen Habermas, and others, I aim to demystify the logical underpinnings of this *noncritical* multiculturalism and thereby produce a space within which the development of *critical* multicultural practices and theories can occur. I attempt to displace *noncritical* multiculturalism by producing a *critical* multiculturalism that functions through a dialectic that is at every step of its own process self-reflexive of the theories, practices, and institutions that produce it. I begin this work in the field of English because English is a traditional discipline, and it is a core academic discipline in the cultural institution that is charged with the production of a homogeneous, monocultural American Subject. This Althusserian big "S" subject defines all "O"ther subjects in relationship to itself and it is both identified and protected by its ability to appropriate those who possess nonvisible markers of difference. This means that those who are physiologically marked as different cannot ever fully assimilate, and this suggests that the definition of American subjectivity needs to shift.

Critical multiculturalism can begin a shift of consciousness, or as Friere calls it "conscientização . . . the deepening of the attitude of awareness characteristic of all emergence" (Friere, 1993: 90). This consciousness allows for an awareness of the contingent and constructed nature of human identities. This awareness can then allow for a concept of the differences that exist between identities to be understood as constructed and contingent, and in this way mutable and transient. Through an understanding of the mutable quality of human identity and the differences that are constructed to keep them locked into certain kinds of relationships students and teachers can begin to investigate the cultural mechanisms that serve to produce and reproduce those relationships. In this way a critical multiculturalism can allow a space within which change can occur in institutions that were developed historically and traditionally out of a logic system that sustains itself through practices that produce differences and support the hierarchization of those differences. These processes result in the production of different values for different kinds of people, values that set people in competition with one another for the positions of privilege as defined by the institutions that promote the competition. The logic that produces this competition also produces racism.

In order to address racism, sexism, ageism, and homophobia in America, the institutions have to change. How is it possible to change institutions that one is actively engaged in supporting simply by his or her very presence within them? In this work I follow advice given to me by American poet Frank Bidart. I had the good fortune to speak with Mr. Bidart while I was a graduate student at the University of California at Riverside in 1994. I told him that I wanted to write a dissertation that addressed the issue of multiculturalism, but that I did not want to write what I perceived to be a standard, antagonistic academic response. I wanted to write something that would open up possibilities and not simply antagonize those with whom I disagreed. Mr. Bidart replied, "find a topic which is not used as a polemic for an alternative which is itself coercive." It has taken me years to understand this comment. To this end, however, I have tried to construct a critical multiculturalism that opens up concepts such as race, difference, power, knowledge, education, and identity in ways that do not simply offer a counterdiscourse to the extant discourse. I attempt to open these categories of human existence in ways that will allow for many alternatives to be designed by many theorists and practitioners for many years. I build on the work of what I have labeled noncritical multiculturalism, and I try to make that connection clear. This is because I find no fault with those practices, theorists, or practitioners. Their attempts are good willed and useful. However, they cannot be the last word. Critical multiculturalism assumes that it will and must meet its own opposition. Through that opposition it can become something else and in this way critical multiculturalism increases the range of its discourse.

Because I do not wish to be coercive I have followed the tenet of critical theory (per the Frankfurt School) as closely as I possibly could. That is, I have tried to be always self-reflexive in my theory. What I strongly suggest in all of the chapters contained herein is that change can come from self-reflexive practice and theory. I argue (and I do argue) that a result of constantly examining where we are theoretically and practically is that we can then conceptualize new relationships between theory and practice that will allow us to change the institutions that theory and practice support.

This work constantly negotiates other borders as well. The research material comes from the discourse produced by composition as well as literary criticism and appropriates work done in the areas of economics, ethnic studies, history, and education.

In chapter one I illustrate the problematic associated with any attempt to present a full representation of the historic topic of multiculturalism. In order to do this properly one might want to devote an entire project to researching the archives of public policy, academic policy, the journals of the social sciences, and more recently, the literature of the "hard" sciences. The conversation has been carried on under so many topics and appears as undercurrent in so many seemingly unrelated issues that I argue that the discourse of higher education in American culture can never be, and has never been separated, from the issue of multiculturalism.

In chapter one, my primary argument is that the university is a cultural institution designed to produce a monocultural population of American subjects out of a multicultural demographic. Necessary in that production process are practices that simultaneously produce difference and efface difference. That is, in order to produce an American subject the institution must produce a model of that which is not an American subject and at the same time produce an American subjectivity that can accommodate any difference. In this chapter, I discuss processes attributable to the university and reproduced at the university through no conscious intent of the individuals in the university that have resulted in the production of a noncritical multiculturalism that continues to serve the institution's larger political function, which is to reproduce a monocultural hegemony. I focus my gaze upon the ways in which the historical development of the discipline of English in the American University, and the practices and theories produced within that discourse community have participated in the reproduction of a monocultural hegemony in spite of a growing participation and presence of those Americans marked "multicultural" in the university.

Chapter two moves toward a full articulation of a critical multicultural approach. I illustrate how a noncritical multiculturalism allows for the presentation of difference that exists outside of the dominant culture and unintentionally reiterates elements of racist discourse. This noncritical multiculturalism has brought into the university the works of previously marginalized writers of ethnic distinction. However, it often traps those writers in a position of subordination to the "traditional" authors of American literature. The newly introduced works are specially marked "Multicultural," and in this way they are specifically not quite American. In this chapter I map the ways in which noncritical multiculturalism relies upon traditional, visible markers of difference, and then conflates those differences with a concept of cultural difference that reinforces the concept of immutable difference. I believe a critical consideration of the ways in which culture and physical markers of difference have been conflated by a noncritical multiculturalism will allow me to approach Appiah's fallow field. Further, I think it is crucial that it be approached. Mapping the means of conflation is the only way we can be certain that if the specter of race is ever erased, the relationship between differences do not continue to be reproduced. As Cornell West has written, "Race Matters." This work is not an attempt to efface race. I want to map the ways in which race has been used as a marker for difference that has been historically valued as less than fully American.

Mapping the ways in which race has served as a marker of negative value is important not only because it seems to transcend time and place, but because it provides a model for the ways in which other differences function. Work has already begun that identifies nontraditionally marked differences that fall low in the cultural hierarchy: disability, age, and (non-hetero) sexuality are currently being defined as fields for study. These markers of difference will continue to be valued as negative until the concept of difference itself is examined and changed.

The concept of American culture needs to be addressed. The historical function of the university is the production of American citizens. That is, it is believed that those who pass through the rigors of higher education are prepared to participate more fully in the political processes that govern America than those who do not. College graduation produces a citizen who is fully prepared to participate. The ideology of a university, academe, then plays a major role in the production of American culture by virtue of the citizens it produces as well as the relationships that are defined between those who attend and those who do not. This process must come under scrutiny because it directly affects the pedagogy practiced in the university. It is through pedagogical approach as well as theoretical posturing that the academy produces and defines what is more, or less, American. In this way, difference is marked, power is protected, and identity is rendered immutable. Part of the strategy of remarking difference is to foreground "white" as a category that is represented as homogeneous, in spite of differences that exist within the category in many works of American literature. An examination of the ways in which these intragroup differences are effaced allows for an understanding of how power is maintained by a dominant cultural group. In chapter three I map out some of these strategies.

Chapter three follows the model of a critical multicultural literary theory articulated in essays contained in *The Ethnic Canon* (1995), edited by David Palumbo-Liu and in the foreword to that work, most succinctly, by Palumbo-Liu himself. In this chapter I analyze Mark Twain's *Adventures of Huckleberry Finn* (1995 edition), Ralph Ellison's *Invisible Man* (1989 edition), Maxine Hong Kingston's *China Men* (1989 edition), and her novel, *The Woman Warrior: Memoirs of a Girlhood Among Ghosts* (1977 edition). I read these texts as American texts as opposed to multicultural texts. This allows for the text to read within as well as against traditional literary criteria and foregrounds the function of the metaphor of visibility. Visibility, traditionally, equals power and invisibility is that which equals powerlessness. This metaphor is a mechanism that has served to maintain the power position of the dominant culture. The texts read in chapter three not only foreground this metaphor but deconstruct it. This work begins a shift in the binary relationship between visibility and invisibility. Through this process of demystification a space is produced within which relationships of power based upon appearance can be interrogated.

A critical multicultural literary theory reads for categories of cultural identity and the ways in which relationships are set up between those identities. This allows for a consideration of the ways in which Anglo-cultural identity is very often effaced, made transparent. Invisibility, or opacity, as a critical multicultural reading can illustrate, is a mechanism that allows a dominant (and predominantly) Anglocentric culture to maintain its power position. In this way the metaphor of invisibility begins to shift. Toni Morrison argues in *Playing in the Dark: Whiteness and the Literary Imagination*, that a Eurocentric, dominant, "white" culture cannot escape defining itself in terms of the "black" American presence. Identifying moments in a text when that defining action occurs makes visible not only the process of appropriation but also the process by which Anglocentric culture maintains its dominant position by maintaining an invisible presence. This is illustrated in the relationship between Tom and Huck and their relationship with Jim in Twain's novel, and it is illustrated through the description of power found in Ellison's and Kingston's works. This allows for an understanding of the power of invisibility and brings into question the function of a notion of invisibility that exists in a position of powerlessness. In going back to the texts wherein we can see this process occur, we can perhaps learn how to demystify those processes and change them.

Chapter four is concerned with the development of pedagogical practices that directly address concepts of power, identity, and difference. I refer to a critical multicultural composition class I designed and implemented at the University of California at Riverside. In this class I attempted to construct a classroom that could allow for the practice of a critical multiculturalism. Henry Giroux has written that any radical project needs "a language of critique . . . [and] . . . a language of possibility" (Giroux, 1988: 31). To this end, I have constructed a pedagogical model that I believe performs the tenets of the theory I have produced. That is, I have attempted to develop a pedagogy that liberates both teacher and student from the bonds of their respective static and monolithic identities, and encourages and models a set of practices that allows them to critically analyze representations of difference. Finally, I hope I have begun work that will allow for the development of pedagogies that can prepare a student for full, critical, and active participation as a citizen, worker, and member of the communities of his or her choice.

In *Theory and Resistance in Education: A Pedagogy for the Opposition*, Henry Giroux discusses the concept of citizenship education in depth. In *A Pedagogy for Liberation: Dialogues on Transforming Education,* Ira Shor and Paolo Friere discuss liberatory education and critical consciousness in detail. No work on the topic of multiculturalism or critical pedagogy would be complete without a consideration of the impact of Paolo Friere' *Pedagogy of the Oppressed.* These works have directly and indirectly informed the concept of critical multiculturalism that I employed in that first experimental classroom and continue to employ and refine in every classroom in which I am a participant.

In the critical multicultural class everything is text, and all texts are read in order to recognize the ways in which difference is constructed, defined, and hierarchized. This allows for the interrogation of the criteria that defines difference, maintains unequal relationships, which are dependent upon a concept of difference, and perpetuates difference as a negative aspect of human identity. In this way the process of mapping the cultural practices through which the conflation of race and culture occurs can begin. This is a crucial mapping process in terms of the "multicultural" students that a noncritical multiculturalism purports to serve. This allows a student marked by physiological difference to see the ways in which he or she is trapped in an inequitable relationship with a dominant culture. It allows an individual to understand that the differences he or she has been made to represent are culturally constructed. This is not to say that it allows one to escape such constructions. However, a critical multicultural classroom is a space within which a person can begin to shrug off the burden of being that which serves to define a dominant culture through his or her presence outside of it, and it allows an individual to begin to construct a response to the practices that allow for such constructions of identity.

Critical multiculturalism relies not only on the development of a theory but also practices that can teach difference—cultural or otherwise—in a self-reflexive way. The practice and theory must always be in dialogue with each other, and the teacher must be willing to participate. This is a theoretical model and set of practices that refuse to simply talk about students. In chapter four I use student voices as critical responses. The self-reflexive, critically literate teacher must be willing to engage each class as a room full of individuals who are equals in an intellectual endeavor. In this way, critical thinking is modeled as well as taught.

Critical multiculturalism can be used as a theoretical tool that can affect not only the academic institution that supports American culture, but because of the semi-autonomous relationship among cultural institutions it can also offer ways in which those institutions can change. This kind of change is a long way down the road I am on, and it may be a destination I never reach. However, the impetus is in a direction that, as far as I can see today, suggests positive changes for the quality of human life in America. Critical race theorist David Theo Goldberg and Cultural theorist Henry Giroux suggest that changes made in the ways in which we (culturally) imagine difference, made manifest in the academy, can result in a "new language" that will allow for the articulation of cultural institutions that no longer need to rely upon practices that oppress and hierarchize individuals. Giroux's critical pedagogy suggests inventing "a new language for resituating teacher/student relations within pedagogical practices that open up rather than close down the borders of knowledge and learning" (Giroux, 1992: 166). This re-situation is important because the changes in culture-wide, meaning-making systems will be produced out of changes made in the meaning-making systems of the public education system through a redefinition of the relationship between teacher and student. They will be contingent on an understanding of the ways in which we participate as individuals in the logic system that undergirds not only our educational practices, but also our cultural and theoretical ontology.

1
Ethico-Political History and the Production of a Noncritical Multiculturalism

American culture is multicultural. It seems that no one would dispute this statement. The demographics show that the population is multiethnic as well as what we currently call multiracial.[1] As a result it stands to reason that the art, language, and religion produced by such a population would be multicultural. The *question* of multiculturalism, it would seem, is purely academic. There is no way around the multiethnic/racial demographic or the very material products of that demographic. What then is there to discuss when the question of multiculturalism is raised in academic discourse? To answer this question it is necessary to take a look at the institution called the "academy." What function does the institution of higher learning in the United States perform? What is its relationship to the culture at large? How does it function to form or inform that larger culture? We also need to take a close look at the academic discourse concerning multiculturalism. How has it been constructed? If we agree that America is a historically multiethnic/racial social organization, why is there a concept called multiculturalism, which logically appears to be placed in opposition to that which is not multicultural in the American academy?

One practical problem with the current conversation concerning multiculturalism is the lack of clear definition. According to the *Encyclopedia of Multiculturalism,* "there is scholarly disagreement about the meaning and purpose of [American] multiculturalism in the academic program" (Auerbach, 1994: 11). The academic discourse concerning multiculturalism over the past decade has been characterized as: (1) canon reformation, (Lauter, 1991; Wolf, 1991), (2) a reformulation of the artistic aesthetic, (Levin, 1992; Simonson and Walker, 1988; Yamada and Hylkema, 1990), (3) an alternate knowledge paradigm for the humanities and the soft sciences, which would include pluralism, (Buenker and Ratner, 1992; Ravitch, 1990), (4) the development of a pedagogy that is focused on a decentralized source of authority (these arguments often question the traditional formulation of cultural identity), (Lu, 1994; Geyer, 1993; Coiner, 1992), (5) egalitarian legislation at the national political level and curriculum development at the university level, (Appleton, 1978; Matsuda et al., 1993), (5) "political correctness" or diversity, which detracts from the traditions of the university (Bernstein, 1994; D'Souza, 1991; Bloom, 1987; Hirsch, 1987), and (6) "a cautionary tale against cultural excess" (Gates, 1993; Suleri, 1993, 17; Chicago Cultural Studies Group, 1992; Erickson, 1992).

Much of the current multiculturalism debate centers on issues concerned with the reformation of the American canon and university curriculum formation. However, there is also an understanding of multiculturalism as globalism. A consideration of this practical problem leads to an understanding of one of the functions a noncritical multiculturalism performs. This kind of slippage disallows a representation of American culture that perpetually and openly negotiates the presence of cultural difference within its own boundaries. Instead discussions of difference can easily shift to that which exists outside the national boundaries of the country. Through a conflation of discussions centered upon differences that exist within the country and differences that exist outside the country, a clear and distinct discussion of the ways in which difference functions in the United States is elided. This conflation functions to protect the integrity of a homogeneous American cultural identity by shifting our cultural gaze from differences that exist within the national identity to a larger consideration of the differences between cultures in general. This is not to say that this larger discussion is not a useful one. However, this conflation of two very different discussions is a hallmark of noncritical multiculturalism that allows it to function as a mechanism of an institution charged with the reproduction of a monocultural hegemonic agenda.

One way to begin to see the ways in which noncritical multiculturalism developed as and continues to function as a mechanism of a monocultural hegemony is through the work of Antonio Gramsci. In *Antonio Gramsci: Selections from Cultural Writings* editors, David Forgacs and Geoffrey Nowell-Smith report that one of Gramsci's prison notebooks (*Notebook 10*) was dedicated to a working out of the philosophical works of Benedetto Croce. They report:

[Gramsci] seizes on the importance of Croce's focus on 'ethico-political history': on culture, the historical function of the traditional intellectuals, consent, [and] civil society. Croce had criticized historical materialism for deifying the economy and treating the ethico-political sphere as a merely phenomenal superstructure reared up over it. (Forgacs and Nowell-Smith, 1985: 90)

From Croce's work, Gramsci developed a concept of ethico-political history as a history that allows a view of the ways in which the institutions that support a culture interact with one another. As Louis Althusser would argue, the institutions that support a culture are in fact intertwined in a semi-autonomous relationship with one another (Althusser, 1971). The history of art, literature, and economics, for example, in any given culture may be read as the history of relationships that exist between ethico-political spheres. The history of the development of English as a traditional discipline in the American university, and the ways in which the apparatuses of literature and composition have functioned, and continue to function, in the University can provide an ethico-political history of multiculturalism. Such a historical perspective can begin to shift the focus from race, which in some ways has been deified in the dialogue concerning multiculturalism, to discussions of difference.

Mapping the production of traditional academic multiculturalism, from here forward referred to as noncritical multiculturalism through a mapping out of the ways in which a variety of ethico-political spheres contributed to that production process allows not only a view of the concept of multiculturalism, but of the institutions that produce it. This seems to have been Gramsci's primary argument with Croce. A focus on only one institution cannot fully illustrate the fabric of a hegemonic structure. The complicity of institutions in maintaining a hegemonic power structure must be established in order to utilize effectively any focused discussion of one particular institution for change.

The historical function of academic, non-critical, multiculturalism in American education was not initially designed, nor has it as yet been redesigned to self-reflexively interrogate its own construction or function. In this way, the well-intentioned usage of the theories and practices developed in the name of multiculturalism have, historically, functioned to perpetuate the oppression and repression those identities that do not serve to promote an image of a homogeneous American culture. In the academy, this is effectively accomplished through the mechanism of liberal and conservative debate. This discourse maintains a tension between the image of American culture and the reality of American culture that does not allow for a critical consideration of the ways in which both sides participate in the repetition of the problems they view as having been produced by those on the other side. In this way, the assimilation and enculturation process continues sans critical critique.

One way the liberal/conservative tension has protected the American university from critical consideration of its own practices is through the conflation of discussions of difference that exists in America that is called multiculturalism with discussion of difference that exists globally that is called multiculturalism. Globally there has been much work done on multiculturalism. Work produced by academics in Canada, Great Britain, Sweden, Switzerland and Australia dramatically predates work done by American academics in many instances. With few exceptions these discussions of multiculturalism have referred to cultural relationships that exist within a specific nation/state boundary (Gunew and Longley, 1992; Rizvi, 1986; Horton, 1993; Ludwig, 1996). For example, much of the work done in the area of Canadian multiculturalism deals with the relationships that exist between immigrant cultural groups and indigenous cultural groups that are present in Canada.

The force of the liberal/conservative debate is such that it seems to have produced a reluctance on the part of American academia to engage relationships of difference that exist strictly within America. This deflective strategy suggests that if change of an ideological nature occurs in one institution, all the other cultural institutions will be affected. Works within one or another of the cultural institutions may struggle against the dominant code or culture; however, the changes that occur from that "alien" performance will have to be accommodated in a way that supports the hegemony before it can be internalized. This seems to be the function of liberal/conservative discourse.

The early debates concerned with multiculturalism in American schools occurred in academic circles concerned with K-12 education, and it has had much iteration there over time. Ronald G. Edwards writes in "Multiculturalism and its Links to Quality Education and Democracy" that multiculturalism is a "basic concept [that] has existed since the 1920s when [primary and secondary] educators started writing about intercultural education and ethnic studies [in order to] orient the populace to newly arrived immigrants" (Edwards, 1993: 12). Edwards's essay attempts to establish a precedent for the current reintroduction of multicultural curricula. It presents a historical antecedent to what some members of the discourse community seem to consider a particularly contemporary issue. However, this essay also provides an historic referent, which allows a view of the academic theory and practice of multiculturalism as a paradoxical means by which the material multicultural reality of the United States was systematically recognized and denied. The "multiculturalism" to which Edwards refers was the practice of introducing "foreign" cultures to the domestic culture of the American school system. This produced (and reproduces) a body of, already assimilated, "American" students in an American institution who need to be educated in the ways of "foreign" students who possess "O"ther cultural training.

The practices to which Edwards refers were integrative practices that refused to acknowledge the multicultural reality of the students already present in an institution that was designed to assimilate cultural "O"thers (other than those marked as "American") into the institution. This characterization of the American public school system illustrates the function of effacing national, demographic, material, and cultural differences presented by a diverse population that already existed within national boundaries by producing a cultural, national "O"ther that exists outside the geographic boundaries of the United States. Everyone already in the institution becomes American by dint of the relationship between non-American and American. Early multiculturalism was the mechanism that allowed for the definition of cultural difference to be that which exists outside of American culture. This mechanism continues to efface those differences that exist inside of national boundaries in the interest of producing a homogeneous, monocultural, national - American - identity.

American identity seems to be the pivot in the liberal/conservative debate concerned with multiculturalism. A multicultural debate that centers on issues of tradition and non-tradition seems to serve to protect the traditional concept of American identity. What does it mean to be an American? What does it mean to have an American education? These are the questions upon which the current liberal/conservative debate is currently focused and upon which liberal/conservative debate has focused since the need for an American identity developed.

In 1788 James Madison argued for the ratification of the Constitution because he believed that the Senate had to be accepted as representatives of a homogeneous, stable, and secure political structure.

He wrote:

> Independently of the merits of any particular plan or measure, it is desirable on various accounts, that [foreign policy] should *appear* to other nations as the offspring of a wise and honorable policy: [and] second, that in doubtful cases, particularly where the national councils may be warped by some strong passion or momentary interest, the presumed or known opinion of the impartial world, may be the best guide that can be followed. (*Federalist Paper No. 63*, 1982: 318, my emphasis)

Madison calls for the "appearance" of a national character that could be accepted by those European nations that had organized themselves around the concept of a national character. The appearance, or representation, of a homogeneous American national character would provide the governing body of the nation known as the United States of America to be understood as "wise and honorable [and stable]." In times of internal crisis, this appearance, now internalized by world powers, could be reflected back to the governing body, and the populace, of America to remind them of what America is.[2]

Madison asks only for an "appearance" of solidarity because as he writes later in this same letter, "however requisite a sense of national character may be, it is evident that it can never be sufficiently possessed by a numerous and changeable body" (*Federalist Paper No. 63*, 1982: 318). The Senate was to be a microcosmic representation of the "numerous and changeable body" that was the United States of America. It seems that Madison believed there was a need to transform a multicultural demographic into a monocultural image. The proposed idea of a Senate was confirmed, and the effort to produce an American culture with which world powers would interact began. This historical moment is where we can locate the beginning of a dominant American culture—a culture that is currently set in a relationship of binary opposition to multiculturalism.

The mechanism designed to promulgate the dominant culture was the institution of higher education. While this institution was at first private and partisan, later institutions such as the common school, the public primary and secondary school, and land-grant institutions of higher learning that were opened for general admissions were modeled after them. Thomas Jefferson was charged with designing the American university. He wrote in an 1818 *Report to the Commissioners for the University of Virginia* that among other things the "objects of that higher grade of education [are] to develop the reasoning faculties of our youth, enlarge their minds, cultivate their morals, and instill into them the

Ethico-Political History 19

precepts of virtue and order" (Jefferson, 1977: 334). Jefferson's model was the mechanism that could supply Madison's Senate with cultural representatives who could perpetuate the appearance of a unified and homogeneous population. It is problematic because it was designed to produce only educated, rich, Western, and Northern European-American males in roles of leadership. It also required the development of a homogeneous set of cultural values that could be institutionalized and transmitted. Historically, these values have been understood as those morals and methods of reasoning associated with Upper class, Eurocentrically trained males. However, in that same report Jefferson wrote:

It cannot be but that each generation succeeding to the knowledge acquired by all those who preceded it, adding to it their own acquisitions and discoveries, and handing the mass down for successive and constant accumulation, must advance the knowledge and well-being of mankind, not infinitely, as some have said, but indefinitely, and to a term which no one can fix and foresee. (Jefferson, 1977: 336)

Jefferson's concept of higher education coupled with Madison's recognition of a "numerous and changeable" populace allows for an understanding of the American university as an institution charged with producing both a citizenry that can serve as representative of a unified, homogeneous set of values, and a dynamic set of values. The homogeneous body of citizens produced by the university is charged with providing the appearance of a unified national character and with protecting the heterogeneous nature of the populace.

It was and is the function of the university to translate heterogeneity into the appearance, or representation, of homogeneity. Jefferson's model provides a foundation of knowledge, which was to be added to and adapted as the character of the nation changed. Each generation of scholars is charged to add "their own acquisitions and discoveries" to the knowledge that succeeded them. However, the knowledge that accumulates and advances is not "infinite" but "indefinite." The originary moment of the liberal/conservative debate that currently characterizes the academic discourse concerned with multiculturalism may be located within the word choice made by Jefferson. Jefferson allowed for a university that produced knowledge that was dynamic within limits and that allowed it to remain a mechanism that produced a student who could be read in terms of a unified, identifiable and "stable" national character.

The curriculum devised by Jefferson does allow for change. It does allow for the recognition of multiplicitous knowledges.[3] However, this ability to change is immediately problematized by the realization that any change that is produced in that body of knowledge can only occur through that body of knowledge. This formulation of the Jeffersonian model illustrates the means by which a liberal faction might rightfully believe that the needs of the multicultural demographic would have to be met. At the same time we can see that the conservative goal of providing a homogeneous cultural knowledge is the function of the American university. The current debates or "culture wars" surrounding multiculturalism illustrate the continuation of the historic struggle between these seemingly binary directives. This kind of cultural negotiation occurs in academic discourse because the academy is the cultural institution charged with producing the *representation* of American culture.[4] Further, English departments seem to be a site where these negotiations can, historically, be clearly read.

In 1862 the Land-Grant Act legislated the beginning of the public university system. These were primarily technical research and training facilities that would become the site upon which, following World War II, the middle manager would be produced en mass. In 1874, just twelve years later, Harvard opened its doors to general admission through the implementation of an entrance exam, and before the century ended (1892), the "Committee of Ten" had convened to produce what we have come to know as the American literary canon.[5] Harvard's model of an entrance exam was reproduced in the public university system, and the canon was implemented as required reading in virtually all public university English departments. The twentieth century opened the academy to the general, multicultural, populace, and Harvard's entrance exam, and the canon, assured the dominant culture of its own representation in all of these academic institutions.

The Harvard entrance exam was used, in part, to determine who was capable of participating in the advanced study of literature, and which students required instruction in composition. (Kitzhaber, 1990: 34-35). In the early stages of Harvard's development of an English department, composition and literature were not, de facto separated. Works of literary merit were used as models and prompts in the "English" classroom because, as Adams Sherman Hill wrote in 1879, "It was hoped . . . . the student . . . would acquire a taste for good reading, and would insensibly adopt better methods of thought and better forms of expression" (35). Kitzhaber writes that by the end of the Nineteenth century, "In a curriculum largely elective, freshman composition . . . had become one of the few courses that every student had to take" (225). Kitzhaber goes on to report that while the study and teaching of composition was considered a suitable academic endeavor well into the 1890s, after the turn of the century composition became coursework taught by "untrained graduate students . . . [and] full-time teachers of the lowest academic ranks" (225-226). Kitzhaber does not offer an explanation for the shift in standing that composition instruction, or as Patricia Bizzell and Donald Bartholomae have expressed it, bringing the student into academic discourse through intensive grammar instruction has undergone. [6]

Several theorists have posited theories regarding the shift in the ways in which composition has existed in the university English department. Susan Miller writes, "[Harvard President Charles] Eliot opposed the notion that 'just anyone' could accomplish tasks previously thought to belong to an elite, but at the same time he wanted to expand the range of students Harvard would address" (Miller, 1991: 50). Miller argues that one explanation for Eliot's desire to open up the university is the growth of a multicultural demographic and the shrinking of the economic upper class. This demographic shift may also serve as an explanation for the shift in standing experienced by composition as a discipline. Miller writes,

The 1893 depression bankrupted 150 railroads by 1894. Wage-cuts and strikes involving three quarters of a million people followed . . . [I]n Milwaukee as in other industrial trade centers, nineteenth-century immigration had resulted in a severe threat to the Anglo-Saxon upper class. A Polish militia unit was formed in the city; its dominant newspaper was written in German. The potential for social unrest gave the "new university" good reasons, by the lights of the state and its traditional Anglo-Saxon origins, for focusing on vernacular literary ideals supported by the "test" of English composition . . . . As if it had been planned by national authority . . . English took its modern shape, in the 1890's. The two pursuits of literature and composition were immediately joined as "high" and "low", advanced and elementary. (52-53)

The "new university" of the late Nineteenth Century in a sense followed Jefferson's model in designating a lower level of instruction for those who were "of promising ability and character" and yet had been burdened by being the product of an "[un]refined home" and a higher level of education which would allow those students of "refined homes" to consider the moral lessons of *belles lettres* (Miller quoting Eliot in Miller, 1991: 51). However, Miller's example also offers economic and demographic evidence for Eliot's need to open the university in order to accommodate the emerging multicultural demographic.

The development of the division between composition and literature allowed Harvard to accommodate the difference brought into the institution by the multicultural masses and still maintain the privileged position of the dominant culture. This curriculum decision allows for the stratification of Harvard's undergraduate population in ways that reinforce the homogeneous image of the dominant culture, and in this way accommodates the representation of difference without openly negotiating difference.[7]

A Multicultural demographic is the material reality out of which the monoculture of America is produced. Recognition of this relationship on an institutional level threatens to destroy a "seamless" American cultural consciousness. The function of the university as an apparatus that produces the image of seamless assimilation, accommodations and enculturation is threatened by any presence that calls attention to this function. Therefore, instead of changing curricula in ways that would acknowledge and investigate the presence of cultural difference in American culture Harvard designed curricula that accommodated cultural difference and preserved the image of the dominant culture as seamless through the production of those who were different. Composition instruction then becomes the site of assimilation through remediation for these cultural others, and literature is the site upon which Americans can critically engage the tenets of the dominant culture.

Harvard institutionalized the practices of remediation and accommodation through which a multicultural demographic might be assimilated into American culture. Virtually, every other educational institution in the country followed Harvard's lead, and the courts codified the assimilative function of the public education system in America during the 1920s. Nicholas Appleton presents as the first multicultural court case in the American judicial system, the 1923 case of Meyer *vs.* Nebraska. In 1923 the Nebraska State Supreme Court decided that "Robert Meyer, a teacher at Zion Parochial school in Hamilton County, Nebraska" could not teach one of his students, Raymond Parpart, to read in German because "permitting foreigners, who ha[ve] taken residence in [Hamilton] county, to rear and educate their children in the language of their native land . . . is inimical to *our* own safety" (Appleton, 1978: 3, my emphasis).

The United States Supreme court overturned the Nebraska decision, stating that while "it would be highly advantageous if all had ready understanding of *our* ordinary speech...the mere knowledge of the German language [could not] reasonably be regarded as harmful" (4-5, my emphasis). The use of the word "our" is poignant in both court decisions. In different ways, both of these decisions articulate the site of a struggle between monoculturality and multiculturality. It also articulates the perspective of a dominant culture. Further, it reinforces the role of literacy and language instruction in disseminating the values of a national subject. The Nebraska Supreme Court assumed a homogeneous set of knowledges and cultural values, which could in fact be threatened if any "O"ther set of knowledges or cultural values were placed in relationship to it. The mere articulation of that kind of relationship was considered dangerous. Any discussion regarding the influence of the German culture on the formation of the American national character was, of course, immediately shut down. We find this train of thought continued in the current dialogue of the conservative faction of multiculturalism's discourse community. The refusal to acknowledge the influence of any "O"ther cultural values, it seems, is the only way to maintain the sanctity of *our* cultural values.

The United States Supreme Court decision in Meyer *vs.* Nebraska assumes that the values and privileged knowledges represented by the use of the English language are, unlike the Nebraska Supreme Court's sentiment, impervious to threat. The values and knowledges conveyed through the use of the English language occupy a position superior to any that might surreptitiously or directly be conveyed through the use and knowledge of a language other than English. This is the liberal argument. By establishing the privilege of American culture, the United States Supreme Court can allow "in" the "O"ther because it cannot do any damage to the integrity of the privileged institution. However, it must be marked as clearly "not-American" and valued as secondary to American practice. This refusal subordinates the role German culture historically played in the development of American culture in order to produce an American culture, which may have been, at most, indirectly informed by German culture. Therefore, what damage could be done by an American speaking and writing German as long as they were equally proficient in their primary language (and culture)—English?

The notion of retaining a dominant culture is very problematic in light of the idea that a multicultural demographic could only produce a multiculture. However, the university as the apparatus charged with negotiating the schisms between a multicultural reality and a monocultural image has, historically, fulfilled this function with relative ease. Those who could be accommodated, appropriated, and assimilated were brought into the culture through cultural acquisition and linguistic coaching. Well into the twentieth century this program was effective. However, in the 1960s the reality of cultural pluralism once again threatened to disrupt the seamless process of incorporating difference into the fabric of American identity. The originary moment for the student unrest of the 1960s can be traced to several historic moments.[8]

What is both surprising and not surprising at all is that the social tensions, that were fomenting in other areas of American culture erupted in the 1960s on the university campus. These events were surprising to those who insist on the apolitical nature of the university. They are not surprising at all once the political function of the university is made manifest. This is illustrated beautifully in the Berkeley campus riots of 1964.

Seymour Lipset and Sheldon Wolin report in their introduction to *The Berkeley Student Revolt: Facts and Interpretations*, "the immediate cause [of the revolt] was an announcement by campus officials that a twenty-six foot strip of land at the entrance to campus, previously thought . . . to belong to the city of Berkeley, was the property of the university and subject, therefore, to existing university regulations dealing with political activity" (Lipset and Wolin, 1965: xi). The presence of "existing university regulations dealing with political activity" suggests that political activity did occur on the campus prior to 1964. The move to reclaim the strip of land heretofore set aside for student political activity suggests a regulation of the type of political activity that occurred on that strip of land previous and up to 1964. Lipset and Wolin state that "[t]his particular strip [of land] happened to be the place where students traditionally conducted political activity" (xi). If there was a tradition of political activity on the strip of land, then there was a tradition of accommodating political activity on the campus. This suggests that Berkeley (at least) was a university that accommodated some types of overt political activity on university property. It was not until the quality of that political activity came into direct conflict with the charge of the university that Berkeley shut down the political activity.

The student protests and the civil unrest of the 1960s was radical. It allowed a moment of clarity wherein, culturally, we could see, as Gramsci has defined it, ethico-political history. In that "arbitrary and mechanical hypostasis of the moment of hegemony" [we witnessed] political leadership . . . [and] consent in the life and activities of the state and civil society" (Forgacs and Nowell-Smith, 1985: 104). The student protests of the 1960s are most radical because those actions laid bare the function of the institution of American education. The protests allowed for the recognition of the political nature of the institution of higher education as a site upon which the production and reproduction of an image of the dominant culture occurs. This was dramatically foreground in the student actions of the 1960s because those actions centered on the absence in the university of those individuals who are not "easily" assimilated into the image of an American — those who are physiologically marked in ways that do not readily allow for their unmarked participation in the collective production of an American identity.

In a document dated January 21, 1968, the Third World Liberation front, a group of protesting students at the University of California at Berkeley, demanded among other things a:

a. Department of Asian Studies
b. Department of Black Studies
c. Department of Chicano Studies
d. Department of Native American Studies
e. [And a]ny other third-world studies program as they are developed and presented

[They also asked for] third world People in Positions of Power . . . [t]hird world chancellors, third world deans and third world people working in the admissions office, [and] that every university program financed federally or otherwise that involves third world communities (Chicano, Black, Asian, Native American) must have third World people in control at the decision-making level, from funding to implementation. (Wallerstein and Starr, 1971: 491-492)

These demands seem both reasonable and radical. The "number of Black students enrolled in college doubled over the period 1964-1970" (Jansen quoted in Henderson and Henderson, 1974: 54). This demographic shift continued until 1971 when "ethnic minorities made up 24 percent of the national college age population, but they comprised only 5 to 6 percent of the total college enrollment" (Henderson and Henderson, 1974: 55). It is no surprise that these Americans were demanding their constitutional right of representation. What was radical about the demands the Berkeley students made was the demand for recognition of the pluralistic nature of the culture that the university was charged with representing. The demands clearly articulate the principle that there must be an equal representation of those groups of Americans marked as "O"ther within the terms of 1964 America.

The promise those student protests held was that the university would be forced to recognize that the "face" of the dominant culture was about to change. The culture the university was charged with producing was no longer a majority of Eurocentric, rich males. It was, in terms of Jefferson's conception of the function of the institution of higher education, time for the succession of knowledge. It seems no coincidence that the student protests occurred simultaneously with the Civil Rights Movement and the Women's Rights movement. Inequitable representation had, by the 1960s, reached critical mass.

On the other coast, the students at City University of New York (CUNY) demanded on February 6, 1969, that the "racial composition of the entering classes of City College reflect the racial composition of the City of New York public school system." More specifically they demanded that "Black and Puerto Rican history and the Spanish language be required of education majors" (Wallerstein and Starr, 1971: 493). The CUNY demands focused on the need for Spanish-understanding teachers in K-12 because those students in the New York public school system were not prepared to enter college. The CUNY students further articulated the same principle; there must be a recognition that cultural entities within the boundaries of the United States require equal representation and participation in the public education system whether they "fit the mold" or not.

The demand for recognition of the culturally pluralistic reality of the United States is a demand that runs in direct conflict with the charge of the American university. The principles of egalitarian education, equitable social justice, and a respect for cultural identities (racial, ethnic, and gendered) are radical ideas. That is, they are ideas the American university had produced an image of but could not practically produce the substance of and still meet its political obligations. The cultural pluralism of the 1960s brought with it another aspect of difference that the concept of American identity was not yet prepared to encompass. The process of meeting the student demands of the 1960s was problematized by the specter of physical difference. Perhaps this is why Harvard could accommodate cultural "O"thers with relatively little civil unrest. The student unrest of the 1960s directly addressed the needs of those students who were ally marked as "O"ther: African Americans, Asian Americans, Native Americans, Chicano/as and, while not mentioned in Berkeley's list of demands, women.

In terms of multiculturalism the CUNY movement and the Berkeley movement are useful because they represent two historical moments in the development of a noncritical multiculturalism. These movements and so many others, that occurred during the 1960s (none of which do I wish to minimize) demanded a representation of an increasing culturally pluralistic demographic, and recognition that education in America is not egalitarian. Both of these principles threaten the "image" of a seamless American culture, wherein everyone is equal and everyone can achieve success through education and hard work. In the movements themselves we can see hegemonic resistance to and struggle against an inaccurate and oppressive image of American culture, and in the institutional responses we can see hegemonic accommodation of those principles. In this Gramscian moment we can see the Madisonian and Jeffersonian models at work. Lipset and Wolin state, "the new generation of students . . . are representative of many in their generation, not just those on a single campus" (Lipset and Wolin, 1965: xii). The student protestors represented not only the students of a variety of university campuses, but the cry of a multicultural demographic for equal participation in the production of the image of America. The Civil Rights Movement and the Women's Rights Movement had to be played out on a university campus because that is where the production of the image of America occurs. The Suffrage and later Women's Movement as well as the Civil Rights Movement can trace their beginnings back to the turn of the twentieth century. However, when those concerns were brought to campus, change happened quickly — if not as efficaciously as one could have hoped. [9]

In terms of the CUNY demands, in 1970, just five years after the CUNY riots, an open admissions policy was implemented. This program of admitting "city high-school graduates to the City University of New York regardless of their grades and [SAT] scores" was both short-lived and a dismal failure. Ed Quinn and Leonard Kriegel in an essay written for *The Nation* write, "few envisioned the extent of the remedial effort [faculty] would be called upon to make" (Quinn and Kriegel, 1984: 414). Not only were the faculty feeling dispossessed, Quinn and Kriegel report "from the moment [the open admissions students] entered CUNY a question hung over them: why had they been allowed to lower the standards of the university?" (414). The students were aware of the extra effort needed on an institutional level to support them, and the faculty was aware of the differences between the new nontraditional student and the traditionally prepared students. Further, the country was watching "CUNY, where education was so glaringly 'free' [it was] said that [academic] standards had been lowered" (414). The connotation of "lower standards" in the CUNY attempt to accommodate "multicultural" students occurred not because it had opened its doors to the multicultural masses, perhaps, but because it had attempted to openly negotiate the presence of difference within the academy. The interpretation of not only opening the academy, but openly acknowledging that such a move had occurred, unlike Harvard's opening, led to the belief that the quality of knowledge in the American academy had somehow been compromised. Privileging the presence of those who were visibly different from the image, which still persists, of an American seems to exist in a relationship of mutual exclusivity with a quality education.

When curriculum changes to negotiate the presence of those students who *appear* to be inassimilable, it is interpreted as a devalued standard of education. The institution that negotiates openly the presence of cultural difference is "not as good" as the institution that "upholds" the standards of the tradition. This is because of the binary relationship between the dominant culture and the cultural "O"ther who should not be negotiated into but who may be accommodated by the institution. The institution that negotiates openly the presence of difference must be somehow "less than" the institution that allows for the presence of difference but does not negotiate with it. Berkeley accommodated the multicultural cry almost immediately and has managed to maintain for the past thirty years an impressive array of multicultural responses. Currently housed at Berkeley are an African American studies department; an ethnic studies department that houses Afro-American studies, Chicano studies, Asian American studies and Native American studies; an English department; a classics department; and centers for the study of Middle Eastern, Asian, and Western European cultures. Berkeley also has the requisite composition program. The opening up of departments outside of the traditional department of English looks (as with Harvard) like an opening up of the university. However, it can also be read as a resistance to a full negotiation of the presence of difference into the traditional arena within which American identity is produced.

The multicultural offerings Berkeley supports are undergirded by a composition program that prepares students for the larger study of cultural difference by firmly grounding them in the linguistic and logical traditions of American culture. It also situates those cultural differences outside of the traditional English department and in this way structurally situates difference as that which exists outside of the Western European tradition. Given the disciplinary boundaries currently in power in the American university, however, Berkeley's model may be the most critically multicultural model now at work. The material realities of multi-cultural programs and departments in the culture of the university, very probably, entail a constant vigilance on the part of those who wish to protect and continue their presence on campus, to constantly consider and renegotiate the relationships that exist between such academic endeavor and the dominant culture of the university administration.

The responses to the demands for a culturally pluralistic and egalitarian system of education made by the student protest movements were accommodated quickly in order to gloss over the hegemonic disruption that the student movements represented, and they were accommodated by institutions, which did not consider, critically, their socio-historical function. This form of accommodation occurred across the country in the form of multiculturalism. A 1991 survey by Arthur Levine and Jeanette Cureton, published in *The Encyclopedia of Multiculturalism*, found that one-third of U.S. colleges and universities surveyed "have some sort of multicultural requirement in their general education as well as ethnic and gender based courses, centers or institutions" (Auerbach, 1994: 11). Levine and Cureton also report that four-year colleges are ahead of two-year colleges in implementing multicultural programs; research institutions are ahead of teaching colleges; public institutions are ahead of private institutions; finally,

> Despite federal regulations, only 36% of the colleges responding to the 1991 survey reported having an active program to attract underrepresented groups to their faculty. While, 40% of U.S. colleges and Universities report that they have faculty development programs specifically designed to improve multicultural activities on the part of the faculty, another 22% report that they include multicultural activities as part of their general faculty development. (13)

In terms of institutional history this kind of a response is fast. It is likewise inconsistent and ill defined.

Berkeley's and CUNY's responses to a multicultural demand for recognition served as models for the rest of the country. They illustrate that the relationship between the university and the larger culture is a relationship between a multicultural demographic and the production of an image of a dominant culture. Both of them attempted to produce curriculum that reproduces the idea that the university can "naturally" accommodate cultural difference. However, when the colleges and universities across the country attempt to emulate the models provided, there is no homogeneous movement. Unlike Harvard these two institutions could not provide a consistent and coherent model for multiculturalism. Following the logic of binarism that holds logical relationships in place such as high and low levels of language skill, and liberal and conservative arguments regarding the ways in which those skills are defined. The East coast/West coast geography of CUNY and Berkeley coupled with the split between literary responses to multiculturalism, and the remedial/compositional responses to multiculturalism represented by the respective schools, should have worked as effectively as did the national emulation of the Harvard split in the previous century. However, it did not work, as the statistics above suggest. This is because the university is charged with the elision of multiculturalism in the interest of producing monoculturalism. The mechanism that maintains this relationship in a state of homeostasis is academic discourse.

The liberal/conservative debate that has ensued has allowed for the dissolution of any coherent conversation regarding multiculturalism through the tension of positing multiculturalism against (outside of) tradition. Berkeley and CUNY themselves serve as markers in this liberal conservative debate. At Berkeley the conservative model of appropriating difference can be viewed in the plethora of "separate but equal" departments and programs that house cultural difference on the campus. At CUNY, the liberal attitude that difference cannot diminish us is modeled by the outright negotiation of difference. With this division comes the further distinction of how each of those schools serve the institutional model. It seems that a school can either follow tradition or be multicultural. The hiring practices, curriculum changes, and student recruiting practiced in some combination and form over most of the country indicates that there is a need to accommodate the multicultural demographic and a desire to maintain a traditional educational institution. From its inception until the 1960s, the American academy has attempted to function as an ostensibly apolitical vault of cultural knowledge that produces an apolitical representation of American culture. The non-critical multicultural reaction to the schism in the apolitical façade of the university can be viewed in a consideration of the ways in which the discipline of English has formulated the discourse of multiculturalism.

Berkeley and CUNY in particular have been used to locate originary moments of two forms of multiculturalism in the English department. Composition theorists cite the CUNY riots as the moment in which they were forced to develop a response to the needs of underprepared students.[10] This discourse has given rise to a growing body of work, which investigates the uses of decentralized authority and multiple voices (fairly radical thoughts in historical terms) in composition classrooms. Berkeley, on the other hand, has become a leader in ethnic studies and multicultural literature. CUNY serves as the historical marker of the university's attempt to accommodate the needs of the remedial masses, and Berkeley serves as the historical model of the university's attempt to address the changes required in an understanding of the academy's higher purpose. These movements themselves have been used as mechanisms that perpetuate traditional stratification in the discipline. Composition serves the basic needs of a multicultural demographic in the process of assimilation, and literature allows for the production of a student who can be taught to be critically aware of the mores and values of the culture.[11]

The student protests of the 1960s demanded equal representation of American cultural groups. This demand resulted in an attempt on the part of the university to offer access to a greater number of American histories. However, as the Levine and Cureton survey illustrates, this process took diverse forms. This variety of responses has allowed the university to assert its accommodation of the radical principles of equal representation while it continues to produce an image of itself as an apolitical institution of the dominant culture. The lesson learned at Berkeley and most graphically at CUNY is the realization that by producing a set of sacred texts, the canon, and by perpetuating the values that allowed those texts sacred status, we teach the values of a "dominant culture," and thereby promulgate the image of a national identity through the suppression of "O"ther narratives even when we (re)present those other narratives. This realization, brought about but not answered by the student movements of the 1960s, finds the academy in a precarious position. How can the academy negotiate the schism between a homogeneous and seamless American culture as produced and perpetuated by the college and university system and the current recognition of the ways in which that homogeneity oppresses, suppresses, and represses a multicultural reality? Here, again, the performances of the liberal/conservative factions of academic discourse come into play in order to preserve the image of the institution.

In "Multiculturalism and the problem of Liberalism," Peter Erickson argues that "the great obstacle to the further development of a multicultural criticism is the conservative-liberal merger in which liberalism duplicates conservative views and loses its identity in the process" (Erickson, 1992: 97). The liberal/conservative tension is not dialectic. Liberalism cannot help but merge with conservatism at this point because both political factions are attempting to preserve the sanctity of an institution traditionally and culturally charged with producing a homogeneous, apolitical knowledge base that is representative of "The American Character." It is the function of both liberal and conservative discourse to configure itself in such a way that it entertains the radical issues brought to the academy and yet preserves the sanctity of the university as a monocultural, apolitical institution. This occurs through the academic discourse that assigns value to the concepts for which recognition is demanded.

A critical or progressive theory of multiculturalism is one that demands not only the presence of difference in the academy, but a reconceptualization of difference that posits that differences be valued equally, and are not hierarchically placed in relationship to that from which it is different. This kind of equality, however, threatens the monocultural character of American identity and the institutions that produce it because they both depend upon the hierarchization of value. A critical multiculturalism produces a comparative model of difference. It asks that not only difference be interrogated, but that the means by which it was defined as a difference be interrogated as well. This allows a space within which that difference can be viewed in a variety of milieus and in so doing that difference may very well be determined valuable. Through this comparative consideration of a specific aspect of difference the function of a concept of difference is, itself, called into question.

For Erickson, the conservative view, represented by people like William Bennett, his replacement, Lynne Cheney, and Allan Bloom, is one that finds any form of multiculturalism to be a dangerous concept because it threatens to change the traditional, Eurocentric model of American culture. This threat has traditionally taken the form of Afrocentrism because the first responses on many college campuses to the plea for the recognition of the country's cultural plurality were black studies programs.[12] As black studies opened the door for greater representation of greater diversity, conservatives realized they could not simply shut the door on such a huge material reality. Conservatives are forced by this material multicultural reality to adopt a more liberal tone. Erickson quotes Lynne Cheney in order to foreground that her version is the same as the hard-core conservatism espoused by Bennett. Cheney writes that the evolution of Western tradition has shown that one need not "look like Plato or Shakespeare [in order to] share in a tradition they helped form — indeed to find their thoughts mighty instruments for reforming and reshaping that heritage" (98). Cheney's model is grounded in an implicit assertion of Eurocentrism that places Plato and Shakespeare at the center of the "heritage" and invites "O"thers to "reshape" it. Erickson points out that this sentiment "does not give sufficient weight to the tension between 'sharing' and 'reforming and reshaping' and hence because it "does not follow through on the implications of reform . . . . [In effect it] promotes the same basic conservatism espoused by her predecessor, Bennett, in the ideal of an intact common culture that requires no major modification" (Erickson, 1992: 98).

The lack of value in Cheney's argument is the result of the similarity of her argument to Bennett's argument. Erickson's argument is that in order to expand the discussion of multiculturalism the values have to be dialectic in quality. The conflation of liberal/conservative ideals as represented by the relationship between Cheney and Bennett do not allow for one idea to resist another and thereby produce another idea. This is the function of liberal/conservative discourse. It is meant to limit the ability to design an[o]ther idea, under the guise of producing ideas. Jefferson charged that the succession of new knowledge be indefinite and not infinite. The liberal/conservative tension maintains and limits the production of new knowledges to those that will serve to reproduce an American citizen and thereby promulgate a definite image of American identity.

Cheney's argument is also problematic because it is grounded in the assertion of the need to negotiate physiognomic difference. One need not "look" like the masters of Western discourse in order to participate in it or change it. This reliance upon physical markers of difference in order to talk about multiculturalism repeats the problem of simple representation. However, it does offer the liberal possibility of inclusion.

Erickson cites Arthur Schlesinger's *The Disuniting of America* as an example of "undue liberal accommodation of the conservative cultural agenda." Erickson argues that "[o]ne basis for Schlesinger's equivocation is his conflation of multiculturalism with Afrocentrism" (99). Schlesinger's argument against multiculturalism is actually an argument against Afrocentrism. It is a thoroughly conservative argument based on the unyielding binary logic that insists on a concept of the center and that refuses to trade one center for an[O]ther under threat of dissolution. Erickson argues that liberal conservatism as represented by Schlesinger stands in the way of developing a liberal response to the multicultural needs of the American culture. He argues that the formulation of this kind of response can best be located in the work of Henry Louis Gates, Jr. who refutes Schlesinger's conflation of multiculturalism and Afrocentrism in his own work.

In "Good-Bye Columbus? Notes on the Culture of Criticism," Henry Louis Gates Jr. argues the Leftist theories that espouse absolute cultural "equity" are naive attempts to posit "that works of culture can be measured on some scalar metric — and decreed, from some Archimedean vantage point to be equal" which is just as bad, if not worse, than the claims of the right that there is some "culture" that is "immanently valuable" (Gates, 1991: 715). In terms of the liberal/conservative debate, Gates's position promises the most interesting discussion of the role the academician/critic plays in designating that which is culturally valuable. However, the call to "let in" works based on "some scalar metric" is not a call from the left. It is a call from the liberal. The call from the left requires the dissolution of the Center. The Berkeley student demands asked for departments of Asian, Native American, Black, and Chicano studies. In other words, they asked for equal representation. This "radical" theory of multiculturalism does not exist in any but a purely theoretical form in the academy.[13] Gates's argument provides an example of the ways in which the liberal/conservative debate functions to maintain status quo. In other words, Gates is suggesting that both positions are problematic and therefore nothing changes. The value of one over the other cannot be established, so no change occurs. Gates also serves as an illustration of the critic's role in the liberal/conservative debate. Negotiating a relationship between the works of previously marginalized authors and the criteria by which a work of literature has traditionally been valued is the work of the critic. Gates's argument that radicals believe there is some "scalar metric" is an argument against an infinite value for works of literary art. It is an insistence upon clearly defined criteria of measuring and hierarchizing the difference between those works. To suggest that there be no criteria is not only ridiculous, but it would place a lot of critics on unemployment compensation. The work of a noncritical multiculturalism serves to assimilate the works of previously marginalized authors into the traditional metric of critical value. The problem is that they very often fall near the bottom because the value of their difference is also traditionally assigned.

The argument over the canon is a renegotiation of the middle, or center, of cultural knowledge, which has historically existed in a space of constant renegotiation between conservative factions and liberal factions. However, until the question of including physiologically marked "O"thers, such as women and men of color, the canon was never in crisis. The additions and deletions made to the canon over the course of its first sixty odd years all served to reinforce the image of a cohesive, stable dominant culture that was made up of Northern and Western European, upper middle class males. In academic discourse concerned with a non-critical multiculturalism, it seems that the problem can only be understood in terms of replacing that center. In "Canon Fodder: An Evening with William Bennett, Lynne Cheney and Dinesh D'Souza," Cary Nelson writes:

For decades literary history has been both written and taught by telling flattering stories about the very tiny percentage of literary texts canonized after the Second World War . . . . In many periods literary history has thus encompassed no general knowledge about what was being written read and debated . . . . To study or teach literary history thus requires us to go well beyond the selective memory embodied in the canon. (Nelson, 1991: 43)

In order to open up the university curricula to courses that would represent the cultural difference contained in the image of an American monoculture, the university would have to recognize the political value of refusing to recognize cultural difference.

In "Multiculturalism: E Pluribus Plures," Diane Ravitch writes that in the discipline of history "the public schools attempted to neutralize controversies over race, religion and ethnicity by ignoring them" (Ravitch, 1990: 338). However, the curriculum could not erase the multicultural aspects of American history. So, Ravitch writes, "[t] he textbooks minimized problems among groups and taught a sanitized version of history" (338). This sanitized version of history is important because without the devalued multicultural presence the monoculture cannot be valued. As Ravitch continues to explain: "Race, religion and ethnicity were presented as minor elements in the American saga; slavery was treated as an episode, immigration as a sidebar and women were largely absent" (338). This course of action allowed Anglo-Americans to be the synchronous presence that is highlighted by the diachronic presence of slavery; the Europeans who arrived first to be the natives who stand in possession against the immigrant newcomers, and the male figure to be omnipresent through the absence of the female figure. These binaries reinforce the privileged position of image or ideology over material reality. Everything different from these experiences and appearances are valued as negative or less than the "originals."

In "Identities in Dialogue," Henry Louis Gates, Jr. asks, "what is this crazy thing called multiculturalism?" (Gates, 1993: 6). In a Foucauldian sense multiculturalism is a crazy thing. It is a concept that exists as both that which can only exist outside the structure of the academy and that, which can never be separated from it.[14] According to this construction, multiculturalism is the material reality out of which the image of a monocultural America is produced. That is, the multicultural reality must be kept separate and yet still work toward maintaining the image of an egalitarian culture of accommodation. It is the recognition of the culturally plural reality of being an American that threatens to destroy a "seamless" American cultural consciousness. It is the threat of destruction that invokes the liberal/conservative discourse, which characterizes much of the academic discourse. The noncritical multiculturalism produced out of a need to accommodate a representation of difference that is maintained by liberal/conservative academic debate functions as a mechanism of accommodation that does not interrogate the relationship between concepts of difference and the institution that produces and values difference, and thereby maintains the historic function of that institution.

The liberal/conservative format of the debates concerned with noncritical multiculturalism serves as a Red herring for conversations regarding the underlying issues of how Americans are represented and how those representations are valued. Noncritical multiculturalism therefore, becomes that which serves to produce and reproduce traditional representations and relationships. A critical multiculturalism recognizes the need to interrogate the relationships that exist to support traditional representations of the dominant culture, those marked as "O"ther than the dominant culture, and the ways in which those differences have been valued.

NOTES

1. Henry Trueba reports in "Race and Ethnicity: The Role of Universities in Healing Multicultural America":

In 1980 there were in the United States 34.6 million speakers of languages other than English, that is 15% of the total population. Of them, 2.6 million were children under age five, and approximately 8 million school-age children. The largest of these groups in 1980 was Spanish speaking, with 15.5 million people (45% of all language minority people). [Dorothy] Waggoner points out that in 1980, the French, German, Italian, and Polish groups had at least 1 million people in the U.S., and that 30 other language groups had at least 100,000 each . . . In that same year 4.2 million children of Spanish language background constituted 52% of the 8 million school-age children living in language minority families. The next size was the French group with 685,000, the German with 594,000, and the Italian with 437,000. Groups that counted between 100,000 and 200,000 were Filipino, Polish, Native American, Chinese Greek and Portuguese. (Trueba, 1993: 1)

2. There is an organization called Netherlands American Studies Association (N.A.S.A.) that recently published a collection of essays entitled *Multiculturalism and the Canon of American Culture* (Hans Bak, Ed., Vu University Press, 1993). The presence of this group and others like it around the world seems to reinforce Madison's argument.

3. Jefferson designed a curriculum similar to that which we now recognize as undergraduate and graduate in that the lower levels of education were meant to be assimilatory and remedial, and the upper levels were designed to teach the student how to problematize the information previously learned. See *The Portable Jefferson,* pp. 337-338.

4. A useful discussion in the ways in which these representations change in relationship to economic social need can be found in Henderson and Henderson. (1974).

5. The Committee of Ten "arranged nine conferences to study and discuss nine different subjects in the secondary school curriculum; none received more publicity that the Conference on English, since one of the chief difficulties the secondary schools were laboring under was the great variety of reading lists specified by different colleges and universities" (Kitzhaber, 1990: 46). Albert Kitzhaber has contributed the fundamental history of the development of the discipline of English in the American university. In this discussion of the "Harvard reports" he reports that as a result of the large number of secondary school students who were failing Harvard's entrance exam, the Committee of Ten convened to set guidelines for secondary

instruction that would allow students to pass the exam. It also served to homogenize the requirements in English at the university level.

6. Both Patricia Bizzell in *Academic Discourse and Critical Consciousness (1992)* and Donald Bartholomae in his essay "Inventing the University" (1985) use the conception of assimilation into a specific discourse community —namely the academy—in order to discuss Freshman composition.

7. We can see the contemporary reiteration of this move to codify cultural values in works like Allan Bloom's *The Closing of the American Mind* (1987) and E. D. Hirsch's *Cultural Literacy* (1987) these books I would argue attempt to recapture the seamless monoculturality that the early canon represented.

8. The Civil Rights Movement, The Women's Rights Movement and the protests against the Vietnam War are all social protest movements that began much earlier and were expressed in other cultural arenas before they became the focus of student protest. Harold Cruse's *The Crisis of the Negro Intellectual* (1967) does a good job of outlining the history of many of the social concerns addressed in the student protest movements of the 1960s.

9. Lipset and Wolin have compiled an interesting and useful set of responses to the activities on the Berkeley campus in 1964. Their response was also surprisingly fast. The publication date (1965) for their 585-page collection containing contributions and reprints from over a dozen different authors suggests a very fast response on the part of the university and the publishing industry. The quickness with which such a voluminous response to the Berkeley "revolt" was produced suggests an institutional need to quickly accommodate the actions and desires of the protestors.

10. Ira Shor, Kenneth Bruffee, Leonard Kriegel, and Ed Quinn are just a few such theorists.

11. Berkeley continues to serve as a beacon of multiculturalism with the 1991 implementation of the undergraduate requirement in American cultures. This is a requirement that can be filled across the curriculum. There are 265 course offerings from which the student can choose. In those listings offered under English there are no composition courses. This reinforces the idea that there is only one way to write or one way to learn how to write. It is assimilative in that although it may employ "multicultural" techniques, the purpose of the class is to teach students the conventions of writing as defined by the dominant culture. Once this process has been completed, the student is then considered capable of considering the issue of cultural difference. At Berkeley, this consideration can occur in a variety of disciplines. This requirement is beneficial, however, it is not critical in that it does not look at the ways in which it masks or at the very least refuses to recognize the ways in which it participates in the presentation of difference at the same moment it effaces difference. All the students become homogenized through their group participation in learning about cultural others. This culture of the college effaces the cultural differences possessed by the individual students. This may be something addressed by individual teachers within these required classes.

12. See Nick Aaron Ford's *Black Studies: Threat or Challenge* (1973).

13. I refer to the work of David Theo Goldberg, Angela Davis, and Henry Giroux among just a very few others.

14. In *Madness and Civilization* Foucault writes that the inception of the asylum was a response to the presence of huge numbers of disenfranchised "workers" who had been displaced as a result of war and was meant to contain that portion of the populace whose presence disrupted the appearance of prosperity the nation wished to project. The asylums functioned to contain the unemployed and transform them, into the employed. Foucault writes:

Let us not forget that the first houses of confinement appear in England in the most industrialized parts of the country: Worcester, Norwich, Bristol; and that the first *hospital general* was opened in Lyons, forty years before that of Paris; that Hamburg was the first German city to have its *Zucthaus* in 1620. Its regulations were quite precise. The internees must all work. (Foucault, 1984a: 132)

2
Reconstructing Multiculturalism Critically

The noncritical multiculturalism that developed historically out of a response to the ever-increasing visibility of the multicultural demographic of the American population served some useful purposes in terms of maintaining the institutions that support the hegemonic power structure. It also allowed for the production of spaces within which the plays of power might be viewed. However, because the practices of noncritical multiculturalism are direct products of an uncritical relationship with the institution that produced them, they are limited in the potential they hold for producing changes in the institution they support. Out of this noncritical multiculturalism, as befits a dialectic process, a critical multiculturalism can be developed.

Critical multiculturalism is a self-reflexive theory that is founded in an interrogation of the concept of difference itself. It is a theoretical model and practices that function comparatively. A critical multiculturalism looks at the relationships between works, authors, deemed different (currently called multicultural) from the dominant image of an American, as well as the relationships between those works and works produced by those who are deemed (somehow fully) American. This critical theoretical move allows for the design of practices that question all of the institutional practices that produce sameness and difference through such procedures as: curriculum change, canon reformation, classroom demographics, affirmative action, legislation, and historical revision. These practices will then produce theories that are responsive to the needs produced by those practices. I use the discipline of English as a model to illustrate the possible performance of critical multiculturalism in chapters three and four. However, these are not the only ways this theory and practice can be performed. Critical multiculturalism can be effective as a rubric that supports the development of myriad theories and practice. It is not a panacea. It does not offer one direction in which the future might move. It is one possibility offered to those interested in changing the oppressive and inequitable relationships that exist among human beings living in the United States at the end of the twentieth century.

A critical multiculturalism attempts to re-evaluate the means by which individuals are locked into unified subjectivities that wed them to cultural identities that an American myth teaches them they can escape. In this work I would like to tie critical multiculturalism to Henry Giroux's use of the concept of "citizenship education" and to the critical pedagogies developed by Henry Giroux and Ira Shor, among others, that are based upon Paolo Friere's model of critical consciousness. A critical multiculturalism is a relationship between theory and practice that is dynamic and, itself, ever-changing to meet the needs of the present day and inform the theories and practices of the present day. In this way it is not teleology, or ontology. It is a critical exercise that informs where we are.[1]

The modifier "critical" is a term that has received wide usage and become less than potent in its wide application. I use the term here as a referent to the work of the Frankfurt school. As Henry Giroux writes:

According to the Frankfurt school, all thought and theory are tied to a specific interest in the development of a society without injustice. Theory, in this case, becomes a transformative activity that views itself as explicitly political and commits itself to the projection of a future that is as yet unfulfilled. (Giroux, 1983: 19)

Giroux continues to point out that the Frankfurt School not only valued theory that acknowledges and insists on its own political value but that these theorists also privilege the development of critical practices that perform those theories (19). The performance of such theory is problematic not only because the theory itself cannot be directly translated into practices that exist within institutions that resist such practice, but also because the demand of such practices, of self-reflexivity, that is required in order to produce such critical theories.

As Giroux writes:

> Notions about citizenship education are complex and rather unwieldy. Citizenship education cuts across disciplines and is rooted in a myriad of political and normative issues. Unfortunately, it has been largely influenced . . . by the culture of positivism, with its underlying technocratic rationality. Hence educators have generally retreated from engaging its most complex issues and have reduced theorizing about this issue mainly to questions of technique, organization, and administration. (192-193)

Positivism assumes a nonproblematic and causal relationship between theory and practice because positivist theories were developed to support positivist institutions. As though citizens could be produced with the same mechanical efficacy as doorknobs. When a theory of education arises that questions positivism itself, implementation of a responsive practice becomes rather difficult. This is because the institutions that produce citizenry have historically obfuscated the production process in order to maintain a mystification of the mechanisms through which that production occurs.

Theories such as critical multiculturalism that demand an interrogation of the ways cultural groups are defined and exist in relationship to one another are reduced to a series of administrative practices that provide the *appearance* of a practical implementation of the theory but cannot in actuality perform such critical theory. This is because critical theory demands the practice of self-reflexivity. Self-reflexivity demands constant change. In order to implement practices that support theories of citizenship education, such as critical multiculturalism, academic institutions would have to exist in a constant state of self-conscious flux. This concept seems to stand in direct opposition to the function the institution was designed to meet. That is, Madison and Jefferson needed an institution that could promulgate an image of a constant and consistent state. It is also problematic because individuals within the institution would be called upon to practice self-reflexivity. This would entail the threat of demolishing an institution that supports them in a position of privilege. A positivist habit of mind immediately cries out, "there is no solution here." The institutions will not change and the individuals, who are supported by them, no matter how good willed they may be, will not abdicate their positions of power.

It seems that abdication of power is all that can change the material reality of the United States in the late twentieth century.

42   The Rhetoric of Diversity

Statistics provided by Holly Sklar indicate that:

The wealthiest I percent [of Americans] owned more than half of all the bonds, trusts and business equity; nearly half of all stocks; and 40 percent of non-home real estate in 1989. The bottom 90 percent owned about a tenth of those assets, except non-home real estate, of which they owned 20 percent.(Sklar, 1995: 6)

The material reality of definite economic class distinctions in this country cannot be ignored. When this economic distinction is reinforced with cultural training (through the accessibility or lack of accessibility to institutions of higher learning), the class distinction is complete. Sklar reports that the classed society of the United States is very clearly racialized:

[A] Black worker with less than nine years experience earned 16.4 percent less in 1989 than an equivalent white worker (in terms of experience, education, region and so on). The gap has widened greatly since 1973, when Blacks earned 10.3 percent less, and in 1979, when Blacks earned 10.9 percent less . . . . While official unemployment rates are high for White young people, they are much higher for Blacks and Latinos.(113)

These statistics are undoubtedly reductionary because they address only the black/white divide. However, they do appropriately reflect the racialization of poverty and the inequity present in the American economic system that the student movements of the 1960s sought to change. These numbers also reflect the failure of the noncritical multicultural practices that were developed as a response to the protests against such inequity. In an endnote Sklar cites Robert Kominski and Andrea Adams, census Bureau report, " Educational Attainment in the United States: March 1993 and 1992 (May 1994). They wrote:

The percentage of Blacks (ages 25 to 29) with four or more years of college has risen from 2.8 percent in 1947 to 11.6 percent in 1980 to 13.4 percent in 1990, while Whites rose from 5.9 percent in 1947 to 23.7 percent in 1980 and 24.2 percent in 1990. (196)

These statistics, positivist evidence of verifiable empirical data, suggest that cultural institutions function to serve the economic needs of the country, and that these needs seem to rely upon the constant production of an underclass to provide a labor class. Further, this underclass has historically been, and continues to be, made up of people of color or those deemed somehow "non-white."[2] Noncritical multiculturalism attempted to redress this problem, but it was limited by it own positivistic approach because the answer is not a mere increase in presence or representation.

Visible difference (race) is the hallmark of a noncritical multiculturalism. The theory and practice that currently constitutes noncritical multicultural discourse foreground physical markers of difference in an effort to make available to students and scholars an understanding of the material multicultural reality of American culture and history. However, when we place an emphasis on physiological traits in order to identify those differences that have previously been effaced by dominant cultural practice, we then inescapably reproduce racism. Racism is an act that identifies and marks individuals as members of one race or another. It is a way of thinking that has historically led to the acts of prejudice and discrimination that noncritical multiculturalism attempted to redress. Although problematic, noncritical multiculturalism has allowed for the development of alternative theories of race. Through the development of pedagogical practices that respond to those theories and the self-reflexive development of theory that responds critically to those practices, a critical multiculturalism can develop.

The function of a critical multiculturalism is to produce a willingness to change within the institutions that support the production of American culture. These institutions are traditionally rooted in racist thinking (at worst) or progressive but elitist thinking (at best). A critical multiculturalism can begin to interrogate the relationships between the dominant culture and those marked as different from it in order to make visible the mechanisms that support inequitable relationships and perpetuate concepts of difference that support those inequities.

A noncritical multiculturalism focuses on issues of racial difference and presents difference in order to efface difference. This focus on race obfuscates the differences that underlie race. Race becomes "the issue of the day" and issues of economic, gendered, and sexual difference are buried, or subordinated, to the issue of race. In this way, a discussion of the relationships that perpetuate a concept of difference as a social construction that is dynamic and changeable is avoided. The concept of race and race relations are deeply rooted in the logic system that supports American cultural institutions. Clara E. Rodriguez writes:

In the United States a racial order based upon a White/not-White classification system evolved in colonial days. This system of classification provided a racist but utilitarian method of ordering society. It was utilitarian because it was a broad, two-category system that, to a large degree, was congruent with, reflected, and helped order the reality of life in the United States (dual labor markets, inner-city and suburban school systems, primary and secondary job sectors, dual housing markets, and so on). It was racist because it was based purely on racial distinctions. The point of reference was the "White race"; one was or was not White. (Rodriguez, 1991: 50)

Rodriguez points up two things here. First, racial distinctions in the United States are traditionally based on a system of binary logic: one is white or nonwhite. This means that any "O"ther racial group is placed in binary opposition to the group marked white. Some can either become part of the group named white or remain forever a member of that group that is not. Some may never fully assimilate because their physical appearance maintains their position as a marked-American. Second, this binary serves as a foundation upon which the economics of the country rests. Rodriguez goes on to point out that in Puerto Rico (and many Latin American countries) there is an alternate form of racial categorization that is defined in terms of biology and cultural status. Rodriguez writes that,

[R]acial classification in Puerto Rico [is] based more on phenotypic and social definitions of what a person [is] than on genotypic knowledge about a person. In other words, physical and social appearance [are] the measures used to classify, rather than the biological-descent classification (i.e., "one drop of negro blood makes you negro") used in the United States. (52)

Although it is problematic in its own way, the racial categorization that Rodriguez outlines is important because it allows for a consideration of economic class as a means of marking difference. The U.S. model assumes that race exists separate from class. This assumption is attributable in large part to the myth that America is a classless society.[3] Rodriguez's model of racial classification is useful in that it allows for a space within which the American model of difference can be considered as a social construction that functions as a mechanism of a larger ideological agenda. This allows for the possibility that the concept of race can change, and that allows for the concept of difference to change; and from these changes the institutions that support the American ideological agenda can change. It seems that in order to change the binary conception of race that presently functions to separate Americans based on visible racial characteristics, the United States would have to give up the notion of "being number one." Such a simple notion as being at the top of the economic world order signifies a deeply embedded investment in hierarchy. Hierarchies are produced from binaries. Can we imagine an America that is "just happy to be a part of the team"? This communitarianism would be a fundamental change in U.S. attitude toward economic security.[4] To change the privileged position of binary thinking would require major change in every aspect of American life.

A review of work done in the discipline of English illustrates that practices implemented in response to theories of noncritical multiculturalism have already begun to generate theories of critical multiculturalism that interrogate the concept of race. However, it is difficult to develop practices that respond to those theories in meaningful ways. This is because the theory addresses a fundamental component of the institutional foundation. To bring it into the realm of interrogation through practical examination poses the threat of demystifying the foundation upon which the hegemonic power structure rests, or, at least the ways in which the academy contributes to the support and maintenance of that power structure.

In an article that is notable for its assembly of cultural studies theorists who are interested in deconstructing categories of race, Ann Louise Keating describes the problematic nature of her attempt to incorporate her own theoretical work on the deconstruction of whiteness into her classroom. Keating's notes that attempts to discuss the ways in which "racialized identity functions, in the construction of an 'American identity',"

often, inadvertently reconstruct[s] it by reinforcing the belief in permanent, separate racial categories. Although they emphasize the artificial, politically and economically motivated nature of all racial classifications, their continual analysis of racialized identities undercuts their belief that "race" is a constantly changing sociohistorical concept, not a biological fact. (Keating, 1995: 901, 902)

This inadvertent reiteration, particularly in the attempt to interrogate the category "white" as a racial category, has led to some "unexpected difficulties" in Keating's attempt to bring this radical theory into her classroom (902).

Keating's essay represents the chain of events that has led to the development of critical multiculturalism. The noncritical multicultural theory of representation resulted in the (re)presentation of racialized difference in practice. This (re)presentation of race allowed for the interrogation of the category race and demystified the racialized quality of relationships that serve to protect and perpetuate the dominant culture. This resulted in the theoretical interrogation of the concept of whiteness itself. However, putting this theory into practice is quite difficult because it threatens to deconstruct all categories of raced identity because it is the foundational category. If we practice the deconstruction of whiteness we practice the deconstruction of all raced categories of identification. This is positive in one way because it achieves the "end" of allowing a view of the function of the concept of difference itself. This is the concept that serves as the mechanism through which race continues to function as a meaningful marker of human identity. However, it also allows for the deconstruction of the hierarchy of identities that college students in particular are attempting to locate themselves within.

Keating's students resisted the deconstruction of the concept of whiteness because "whiteness has functioned as a pseudo-universal category that hides its specific values, epistemology, and other attributes under the guise of a nonracialized, supposedly colorless, 'human nature'" (Keating, 1995: 904). In other words the practical implementation of such theoretical notions as the situatedness of "white" identity works against every reason the student attends the university. Keating's students are attempting to climb the proverbial ladder of success. By asking them to interrogate and critique the identity that sustains and perpetuates not only the ladder but also the justification for the ladder shifts the value of the ladder. Keating writes, "As Henry Giroux suggests, 'whiteness,' domination, and invisibility are intimately related . . . . [W]hiteness functions as a historical and social construction…that secures its power by refusing to identify itself" (905). Students attend university to rise to a position of relative power within the power structure provided by invisible whiteness. To ask them to deconstruct it asks them to revalue every aspect of their identity. Further, it brings into focus the role of the university in promulgating the goal and the identity.

Keating's essay continues to investigate useful ways of constructing an interrogation of whiteness, which is valuable. However, another value in her essay is that it foregrounds the problematic of instituting practices that respond to critical multicultural theories. In terms of a noncritical multiculturalism, it seems that a causal relationship between a theory that advocates multiple subjectivity and a set of practices developed within an institution that paradigmatically produces unified American subjects would be problematic. The assumption that one can inform the other in any effective way leads to practices produced in response to theories that fail to theorize the institution that produced them. As a result, the praxis and theory can only reproduce the functions of the institution that produced them. This suggests that the theory and practice of noncritical multiculturalism are not radical departures from Eurocentric tradition, but are mechanisms of that tradition. In other words, a noncritical multiculturalism was theorized to function as a mechanism of a monocultural institution of assimilation. The practices that were developed out of that theoretical moment can only perform accommodation and assimilation because the relationship between the theory and practice and the institution that produced them was not considered.

If the institution is charged with producing a unified American subject, how does it implement a set of practices that are produced out of the recognition that such subjectivity has historically been used to oppress and repress "O"ther identities? How can an institution charged with the production of a monocultural subject meet that charge through the use of practices that are developed out of theories of multiplicity? In the introduction to *The Location of Culture*, Homi K. Bhabha writes:

The move away from the singularities of 'class' or 'gender' as primary conceptual and organizational categories has resulted in an awareness of the subject positions—of race, gender, generation, institutional location, geopolitical locale, sexual orientation—that inhabit any claim to identity in the modern world. What is theoretically innovative, and politically crucial, is the need to think beyond narratives of originary and initial subjectivities and to focus on those moments or processes that are produced in the articulation of cultural difference. (Bhaba, 1994: 1)

Noncritical multiculturalism began the move away from the need for a homogeneous American subjectivity. However, it has not been able to call into question the institutions that have produced those conceptual and organizational categories. This is because it serves to reify the image of homogeneity through the embrace of difference. In this way "singularities" of difference are effaced and so are the practices that produce them. However, the change has begun. We have already begun to think beyond the originary moments in which these identities and relationships were produced.

Critical multiculturalism can produce the tools that can evaluate the cultural institutions that produced them. This is difficult work because each and every citizen of the United States in some way participates in the maintenance and perpetuation of these institutions. Such interrogation requires that those of us who are fortunate enough to participate in cultural institutions at levels that allow us the opportunity to be actively self-reflexive must do so. In this way self-reflexivity is modeled, and as Keating's classroom model suggests, these practices can be repeated by students who will take these practices into other institutions at other levels of existence. This is not an idealistic notion of how the academy might work. It is to suggest that the changes have already begun to happen, and both theoretical and practical responses are required.

When theories of multiplicity meet the institution charged with homogenizing and controlling multiplicity, the practices of the institution hold sway. Bhabha writes "It is radical perversity, not sage political wisdom, that drives the will to knowledge of postcolonial discourse" (Bhaba, 1994: 212). Nevertheless, it is "sage political wisdom," or self-interest, that keeps institutions running. Institutions may provide a place for "radical perversity['s]" will to knowledge, but the practices that pragmatism has put in place to ensure the viability of the institution are slow to change in response to the radical call.

There is a lag time between radical theoretical communication and practical implementation that suggests that there may be a causal relationship, but the process functions more dialectically. Through a recognition of this dialectic, which functions to disrupt the perceived binaristic cause/effect relationship between theory and praxis, we may gain insight into the ways in which the relationship between radical theories of multiplicity and practices of noncritical multiculturalism are not causal through a brief consideration of the relationship between feminism and the academy.

Lynn Worsham provides an opportunity to consider the relationship between the production of a "radical" theory and its practical implementation in the university. Worsham discusses the problematic associated with attempts to adapt the theoretical works of French feminists to the practices of the writing classroom. Her discussion of Écriture feminine allows one to draw some parallels between the radical work of French feminism and the work that has been done to produce a critical multiculturalism. She writes:

Although we can observe important differences among Kristeva, Cixous and Irigaray they share some common concerns[:] to put into discourse what dominant discourse has relegated to meaningless-ness—the feminine, the body, desire, emotion, sound, voice, rhythm, contradiction—they are not simply theorizing Écriture feminine as the opposite of phallocentrism . . . . Instead they reverse phallocentric logic to draw attention to its arbitrary privilege, its historical contingency. (Worsham, 1991: 92)

Worsham posits a reading of the French feminists as those who theorize a discourse that would illustrate the ways in which the feminine has been made an absence in the male discourse that valorizes all it represents as *True* and *Universal*. One of the aims of critical multiculturalism is to bring the category of racialized subjectivity into the theoretical ring. Theorizing reading practices, writing practices, hiring practices, and political practices, illustrates the ways in which a "white" literary tradition has used the presence of racially marked "O"thers in order to valorize whiteness as True and Universal.

Worsham points up the problem with instituting practices that represent radical feminist theory. She argues:

> One of two things would happen. Either composition would neutralize the radical potential of Écriture feminine in an effort to appropriate it to serve the current aims of the profession and, beyond this, the university, or Écriture feminine would cast such suspicion on the whole enterprise of composition studies as an accomplice of phallocentrism that composition would be transformed beyond recognition. (Worsham, 1991: 94)

In just this way, theories of noncritical multiculturalism have been interpreted by the university into practices that serve to carry out the institution's charge as an agent of homogeneity. The use of noncritical multicultural theory, like feminist theory, has not been seamless in composition studies. The rupture between theory and practice occurs because there is an institutional process that affects both the theory and the practice. This suggests that theory is not the privileged term in a process that has previously held theory as the informing force. It also suggests that practice may not occupy as passive a position as practitioners have been led to believe.

It appears that when the theory and practice are noncritically formulated due to institutional policy and procedure, they may even become obverse negations of one another. For example, when teaching a "traditional," noncritical multicultural composition class, the standard practice is to use narrative written by a previously marginalized author in order to accommodate the interests of students who may belong to the same, or a similar, cultural group, and to inform students of the dominant culture of the experiences of the cultural group represented. On a theoretical level this is a useful if problematic practice. However, in using this text to implement writing instruction the students will tend toward using the representative text as a model. Very often the narratives of previously marginalized authors do not conform to traditional academic convention, so when the student hands in a paper that emulates the characteristics of the model, he or she gets an unsatisfactory grade. The conversation, which occurs at this point, reveals the function of the representative text to be a representation of difference. The teacher can at this point explain this function and neutralize the radical presence of the previously marginalized text or he or she can call into question the traditions of the academy. Ideally, in traditional terms, the teacher will find a way around the issue.

Mapping this circumlocution is a theoretical interest, and a practical necessity, for the critical multiculturalist. Jurgen Habermas writes:

> Theories that in their structure can serve the clarification of practical questions are designed to enter into communicative action. Interpretations that can be gained within the framework of such theories cannot, of course, be directly effective for the orientation of action; rather, they find their legitimate value within the therapeutic context of the reflexive formation of volition . . . . The inhibitions to communication that have their origin in the structures of the system, themselves become a problem to be clarified theoretically. (Habermas, 1973: 3-4)

Habermas posits the probability that while we can theorize practical problems we cannot practically address theoretical issues because the nature of cultural practice is to institute and maintain institutions that do not desire or accommodate self-reflexivity. We cannot (now) reasonably believe that a theory can produce practices that will act out theoretical desire. Habermas suggests that our theories must produce "volition." This term seems to imply the need for a "will to change" that will allow the institution the desire to reconfigure itself in a way that will both allow it to remain as a functioning entity and accommodate the practices devised in response to radical theory.

We can see the need for a volitional quality of response in conceptualizing critical multiculturalism in the language used by academics attempting to implement those practices. Most advocates posit multiculturalism as that which resides outside or against the discourse of the Academy, and they therefore set it in opposition to a center or a central discourse. Min-Zhan Lu analyzes the oppositional quality of discussions of multiculturalism. Lu writes that images of "grabbing" and "import," used to discuss the implementation of multicultural classroom practice, depict "multiculturalism" as a construct whose "import,"

> Meanings, implications and consequences [are] available only to those willing to expend the energy to "grab" it: to search, envision, grasp, articulate and enact it. [Further] these images conjure up the act of importing—of bringing in—perspectives and methods formerly excluded by the dominant institutions. (Lu, 1994: 442)

Lu suggests that this discourse is symptomatic of an academy that believes in an "academic discourse [that is] discrete, fixed and unified" (442-443). It is this privileged, "fixed, discrete and unified" discourse that cannot accommodate a critical multicultural theory that seeks not to displace it entirely but to recontextualize it as one discourse among many. The situation Lu describes does not indicate an impossibility of introducing the texts of marginalized individuals into the academic discourse community. However, it does indicate that these texts can only be introduced after they have been negotiated and hierarchized (valued) within the discourse community. This is what happens to the multicultural text in the noncritical multicultural composition classroom. It is a "good" representation of lived experience, but it is a "bad" representation of academic writing. Its value, in the context of the academic classroom is its difference alone.

Min-Zhan Lu's work begins to map out the ways the institution struggles against the change. In terms of the current configuration of the academy, either multiculturalism is made to fit into the paradigm of a Eurocentric educational system or it does not exist in the institution. This is illustrated in the institutionalized noncritical multicultural response to the demand for equal representation. The liberal/conservative debate that makes up a large portion of the discourse concerned with multiculturalism in English effectively maintains the traditional curriculum while it separately accommodates the multicultural "O"ther. Elsewhere on the campus there are separate programs and departments of ethnic studies or minority group studies that struggle for funding. There is no concession on the side of the institution that there may be another model for conceptualizing social, cultural, or personal identity. There is a lack of reciprocity in the relationship between academic discourse and any kind of multicultural practice: the former frames the latter but the latter does not (yet) affect the former.

In "On the Subjects of Class and Gender in 'The Literacy of Letters'," Linda Brodkey offers an illustration of the lack of a volition to change through a discussion of the way "educational discourse" privileges unified subjectivity. Brodkey posits that because educational discourse allows for a "satisfactory" subject position for the teacher, the teacher will struggle to maintain it.

She writes:

> The same way you don't resist racism by denying that racism exists, but by confronting it in yourself and others, teachers cannot divest themselves of those vestiges of authority that strike them as unproductive by ignoring the institutional arrangement that unequally empowers teachers and students. (Brodkey, 1989: 129)

This problem foregrounds the relationships between theory, institutions, and praxis because it illustrates that even when the teacher examines his or her privileged position it cannot be escaped. The teacher is contained by the practices of the institution in a position of relative privilege. One small example of this dilemma is that no matter how the teacher decentralizes authority in the classroom he or she will always give the final grade. Brodkey's work illustrates the theoretical step of "think[ing] beyond narratives of originary and initial subjectivities" (which Bhabha advocates) in order to "clarify practical questions" through theoretical communication (which Habermas discusses). This conversation, however, will not have a practical effect until the teacher has allowed him or herself to accept the "satisfactory position" the institution has assigned. This allows a teacher to begin to question the ways in which the institution currently prevents the teacher from functioning in any other than that privileged role. This is a Catch-22 that composition theorists such as Brodkey, Bruffee, Elbow, and Shor have spent their careers trying to untangle. The critical multicultural teacher is, just like every other teacher, a mechanism of the institution. What I suggest here, and I believe Brodkey's argument supports this suggestion, is that a critical multicultural teacher must function in a self-reflexive awareness of his or her relationship to and with the supporting institution.

Brodkey's essay describes a writing program where reentry level women in a basic writing course enter into correspondence with teachers in the basic writing program. The writing problems that surprised Brodkey were not located in the student letters but in the letters written by the teachers. She posits that the teachers were resisting any representation that did not meet the culturally accepted role of teacher, in spite of their efforts to the contrary. I suggest that this phenomenon reveals a resistance to a recognition of the multiple subjectivities of both the teachers themselves and the students, as well as what Brodkey posits as an "interruption" of the unacknowledged, privileged position of the teacher that is supported and encouraged by the institution. This interruption precedes recognition and therefore can only exist as a theoretical possibility that ruptures the writing practices of the teachers.

In the beginning of the program, "[the teachers'] letters were replete with the desire to represent themselves as students of writing pedagogy" and thereby to place themselves on an equal footing with their student correspondent (Brodkey, 1989: 129). Very soon, however, Brodkey reports "[t]he teachers exercise[d] their authority infrequently, but decisively, whenever one of their correspondents interrupts, however, incidentally, the educational discursive practice that treats class as irrelevant to the subjectivity of teachers and students" (1989: 130). This erasure of classed difference occurs not because any one of the teachers in the experiment is elitist or working out of ill intent. It occurs because the institution within which they function is constructed in such a way that they are trained to resist any acknowledgment of class, gender, sexual, or ethnic difference. Brodkey's interrogation of this aspect of the academy is quite useful in opening up a space within which the resistance of institutional practice against theoretical change can be viewed. Brodkey's essay describes interruptions "[t]elegraphed by linguistic and/or discursive lapse . . . that signals the teachers' unspoken commitment to a classless discourse" (Brodkey, 1989: 130) This provides an example of the ways in which individual teachers perform academic insistence on a unified subjectivity and the hierarchy of those subjects within an institutional structure that administratively insists on the recognition of difference and yet academically refuses to recognize those same markers. Once the student is admitted into the institution and enters the classroom he or she becomes a homogeneous student as defined by the differences between the identity of "teacher" and the identity of "student." Outside of that academic distinction it seems that the only difference appropriate for academic discussion is racial difference. Class, gender and sexuality cannot be addressed.

The teachers in Brodkey's essay were incapable of articulating their resistance to the specter of classed difference. This inability effectively effaces the differences between members of the class and focuses on the difference between the student and the teacher. This process, or lack of process, maintains the teacher's privileged position in the classroom, and foregrounds the ways in which difference that is not posited in a traditional form can only exist as a theoretical possibility that cannot be accommodated by the practices of the institution.

The women, in Brodkey's study disrupted the educational discourse of the classroom by attempting to articulate the multiple identities they inhabited both in and out of the classroom. Further, they attempted to elicit acknowledgment of some comparable experience on the part of the teacher. In this way issues of class, primarily, were introduced into the discourse of the classroom. Because class is not traditionally marked, that is, marked physiologically, it is difficult for the teachers in Brodkey's essay to articulate a response to it. In this way nontraditionally marked aspects of difference are not addressed. Conversely, traditionally marked difference is articulated and articulatable in ways that maintain those unmarked categories of difference.

In chapter one, Lynne Cheney was quoted as having presented a model of multiculturalism that was implicitly based upon physiological difference. Cheney wrote, "one need not look like Shakespeare or Plato" to participate in the tradition that "they" founded. Cheney's reliance on a physiological marker of difference repeats the same racist logic a noncritical multiculturalism purports to eradicate, and illustrates the absence of any interrogation into the ways in which the tradition she invokes was constructed. This construction of difference allows for the appropriation of difference by the institutional practices of "reshaping" and "reforming" which allows for the reproduction of the "O"ther as that which cannot be accommodated by traditional structure but must necessarily change it. This idea of changing the traditional structure may not be a bad one. However, as Habermas has pointed out, the institution does not see change as a positive move. Therefore, those who wish to change the institution are not valued as positive in institutional terms. [5] Cheney glosses over that reality.

Current noncritical theories of multiculturalism do promise

> new opportunities to rewrite the politics of representation around race and difference by deconstructing in historical and relational terms not only the central categories of "Otherness," but also the dominant discourses and representations that secure "whiteness" as a universalizing norm. (Giroux, 1993: 101; see also Young, 1990; Dyer, 1988; hooks, 1990)

However, this deconstruction cannot (yet) occur effectively at the level of practice. Theory, as Habermas writes, and Keating's essay illustrates, must first influence volition. We must theorize the value/valuelessness of traditional markers of difference before we can begin to implement practices that will revalue those marked in such ways.[6] The value of a concept such as race is that it provides an essential and visible marker of difference that does not require any further interrogation of the marker itself. This allows for differences that exist within the "homogeneous" dominant culture to remain unmarked and invisible, and also allows for the illusion that there is something inherently similar among those unmarked that allows them to occupy their privileged positions within the dominant culture and relegates those physically marked "O"thers forever to identities that can never completely assimilate into it. bell hooks writes of classroom discussion wherein:

There have been heated debates among students when white students respond with disbelief, shock, rage, as they listen to black students talk about whiteness, when they are compelled to hear observations, stereotypes, etc., that are offered as "data" gleaned from close scrutiny and study. Usually, white students respond with naïve amazement that black people critically assess white people from a standpoint where "whiteness" is the privileged signifier [as opposed to signified] . . . Often their rage erupts because they believe that all ways of looking that highlight difference subvert the liberal belief in a universal subjectivity (we are all just people) that they think will make racism disappear. (hooks, 1992: 167)

The students in hooks's class are practicing the strategies that maintain their positions in the dominant culture. To find difference among them is to deconstruct the similarity that allows them an inscrutable position in the dominant culture. The dominant culture as hooks's essay points up is the culture that delineates, defines, categorizes, and hierarchizes difference that defines that "O"ther than itself. Scrutiny invokes the liberal mechanism that protects the dominant culture by allowing those who represent it to efface differences among themselves. The conservative mechanism reproduces and (re)presents those similarities by extending the reach of the dominant culture through the production of those of are "like" those in the dominant cultural group through the label of "multicultural." The liberal/conservative tensions that maintain institutional praxis and adapt radical theory serve to protect the institution by constantly shifting the gaze away from the institution, usually toward the "O"ther whose mere presence threatens to change it.

Stuart Hall has written that the deconstruction of racial categories of identity currently occurring in theoretical discourse amounts to "the end of the innocent black subject"—and, I would add, any traditionally marked subject. What is "[a]t stake here is the recognition that ' 'black' is essentially a politically—and culturally—constructed category, which cannot be grounded in a set of fixed transcultural or transcendental categories' " (Hall quoted in Giroux, 1994: 37). This insight means that to perpetuate the concept of "black" as a race—a fixed set of essential characteristics—we must continue as a culture to perform "blackness." It seems that having called "blackness" into question as a nonessential performance of subjectivity, has called the category of "whiteness" into question as equally nonessential and performative. When this occurs, racially based subjectivities disintegrate and subjectivities, which have historically been secure in their privileged positions through their "essential" differences from the non-privileged, are threatened. At this point the cultural institutions that have been produced and perpetuated by a logic system that requires the binarisms that racial difference makes manifest (currently) are endangered. When racial subjectivity is deconstructed the cultural institutions that support racial subjectivity will also deconstruct. So, it appears the choices are: maintain the myth of racial subjectivity and the binary logic that supports such hateful praxis and theory; work to erase racial subjectivity as a cultural reality and allow the cultural institutions that support racial subjectivity to collapse; or develop theory that can produce a volition to change and practices that can begin to interrogate the logic system that supports such identifications in order to begin to rework the institutions that currently support such a logic system in ways that will allow them to become cultural institutions that can accommodate, support, and encourage multiplicitous realties and equities.

A critical multiculturalism then must produce theory that can bring to cultural awareness the constructed and performative nature of our subjectivities and produce a volition to change. Otherwise the concept of fluid subjectivity will simply be appropriated by the hegemonic power structure. Henry Giroux points out that:

right-wing Whites in America now echo a view of difference not as a marker for racial superiority but as a signifier for cultural containment, homogeneity, and social and structural inequality . . . . [D]ifference is removed from the language of biologism and firmly established as a cultural construct only to be reworked with a hegemonic project that connects race and nation against the elimination of structural and cultural inequality. [This is a practice that] displays difference in order to displace it within a hegemonic project of national unity. (Giroux, 1994: 33)

Current discourse regarding difference allows for racialized difference to be understood as a social construct. However, it is a concession that is made in an attempt to recontain the concept of difference within a discourse of national unity. Moreover, the shift from an understanding of racial difference as a biological reality to an understanding of racial difference as a social construct without a discussion regarding the logical and sociological mechanisms that allow for such a shift allows for a conflation of racial difference with cultural difference and perpetuates the same problematic.

Henry Louis Gates, Jr. illustrates how noncritical multiculturalism can be "reworked" as a hegemonic practice that perpetuates an understanding of difference that relies upon relationships of inferiority and superiority. He writes, "multiculturalism is frequently used in the popular media as a substitute for the earlier designation multi-racial." Using an example of a "Benetton-style Ad with, say, black and white and Asian children together as 'multicultural' [Gates asks] [d]o these children . . . in fact represent different cultures"? He argues that cultural traits, in the case of these children, are "as opposed to physiognomic traits . . . obviously undiscoverable" (Gates, 1993: 7). Gates argues that by presenting these children as multicultural, this kind of advertising reiterates the racist philosophy that physiognomy equals cultural difference, and conflates what has traditionally been recognized as a racial marker of difference with the concept of cultural difference. This conflation produces an effacement of the traditional marker—race—to reproduce a concept of difference that, like physiological difference, cannot be altered primarily because the source of the difference remains unexamined. This procedure reinforces difference while displaying difference, and "[c]ulture is [then] conceived along ethnically absolute lines, not as something intrinsically fluid, changing, unstable, and dynamic, but as a fixed property of social groups" (Giroux quoting Gilroy, 1993: 98-99). Just as the discourse of the academy is "discrete, fixed and unified," each "O"ther cultural identity is then posited as a "discrete, fixed, entity." Each group then becomes invested in maintaining its own discrete, unified identity and in this way does not multiply the possibility of personal identities but sets up a system wherein one must choose one identity over an[O]ther. [7]

Institutionally, the practices developed out of a noncritical multiculturalism attempt to "erase difference" by presenting difference. Noncritical multicultural practice takes the form of multicultural readers (who are multicultural because they represent previously marginalized ethnic groups), multicultural classrooms (that are multicultural because they contain students who represent previously marginalized ethnic groups), and multicultural texts (that are multicultural because they were written by an individual from a previously marginalized ethnic, or about ethnic group experiences that are "O"ther than those experienced by those living within the confines of the dominant culture). These practices conflate the concept of physical "O"therness with the concept of cultural difference, just as the Benetton-style ad (to which Gates referred) does, and they reinforce the concept that these texts, and students and authors, can only be recognized as that, which is not of the dominant culture. They are multicultural, and therefore somehow not quite (unhyphenated) American. In terms of the conflation of multiculturalism and globalism, difference is situated safely outside the parameters of American identity and therefore the dependence upon the physical marker of difference is not so great. However, within the parameters of American identity, race is a crucial marker of difference.

The mere introduction of difference into a classroom may only reinforce traditional concepts of difference. It cannot revalue difference because the source that defines value has not been called into question. Gates closes "Good-bye Columbus" by writing that we cannot be content with "the multiplication of authorized subjectivities . . . rewarded in virtue of being materially deprived." He hopes for a "rethinking [of] the larger structures that constrain and enable our agency" (Gates, 1991: 725). In "Beyond the Culture Wars" he ends with the hope that "a multiculturalism that can accept its limitations might be worth working for" (Gates, 1993: 11). A critical multiculturalism strives to interrogate the deconstruction process inadvertently set in motion by non-critical multiculturalism to investigate the ways in which concepts such as race and difference function to maintain a cultural hegemony that seems incapable of investigating itself. It also seeks to provide the volition to change hegemonic practice. An argument for the attempt to produce such volition is that it is inevitable that the structure of American culture will change as a result of the work done by a non-critical multiculturalism. Critical multiculturalism offers the possibility of changes that include the precepts upon which the country was theoretically founded. Equality, liberty, and justice are the precepts of the American identity. However, the practices of American institutions have defined these precepts in ways that limit access to them. The schism has been made manifest. Critical multiculturalism offers a means of using the atmosphere of change that is occurring at this historical moment to radically shift the ways in which we have conceived of the precepts of American identity. This can be done through a "shift in locations" (hooks, 1991: 177).

In "Representations of Whiteness" bell hooks quotes Gayatri Spivak in calling for a "shift in locations." She writes:

In the Post-Colonial Critic, Gayatri Spivak calls for a shift in locations, clarifying the radical possibilities that surface when positionality is problematized. She explains that "what we are asking for is that the hegemonic discourse, and the holders of hegemonic discourse, should dehegemonize their position and themselves learn how to occupy the subject position of the other." [hooks comments, a]s critical intervention it allows for the recognition that progressive white people who are anti-racist might be able to understand the way in which their cultural practice reinscribes white supremacy without promoting paralyzing guilt or denial. (hooks, 1992: 177)

A critical multiculturalism can provide the "shift in locations" called for by hooks and Spivak, and at the same time that it multiplies "authorized subjectivities" it allows us to rethink the larger structures that constrain us (Gates, 1991: 725). Racism is the first "larger structure" that needs to be rethought.

David Theo Goldberg presents three fundamental factors that must be addressed in any theoretical consideration of the possibilities for constructing "appropriate counterdiscourses to racism." They are:

Radical alteration of socioeconomic determinants [that allow for hierarchization of social classes, and the racial implications of that segregating practice]; a transformation and extinction of the formal components [of racial discourse], its grammar and language; and [an] alter[ation] of subjective practice . . . which amounts to abandoning racist discourse on a conscious psychological plane. (Goldberg, 1990: 313)[8]

Goldberg's first point reinforces hooks's, Spivak's, and Gates's positions, that a consideration of the classed culture of American society can occur when an attempt is made to reconfigure the ways in which race functions in America. A noncritical multiculturalism focuses on racial difference alone as the primary cause of social dis-ease. The perpetuation of this idea perpetuates the premise that racial difference exists as a universal determinant that cannot be affected by any other determinant. In terms of noncritical multiculturalism this logic is manifest in the idea that if we learn about the "O"ther we will learn to respect the "O"ther. However, because this logical sequence reinforces the idea of unchangeable difference once again those marked as different must and will remain in the historical position of he or she who is different and therefore less valuable than he or she who defines them as such. They remain different or "O"ther and even with the best outcome they are valued as such. This allows a space in which all the negative connotations the concept of difference or "O"ther now carries can remain intact and unquestioned.

The alteration of the racialization of poverty and the repression of the reality of a classed American culture is crucial to overcoming current racist practices. Any set of practices that uses, as the sole measure of discretion, the concept of race is inherently, if unconsciously, racist. A noncritical multiculturalism attempts to rectify such schemata with the introduction of an understanding of difference through a presentation of difference. However, what is required is a new way of understanding difference. It is a catch-22 to try to defeat racist thinking by presenting difference defined exclusively in terms of race.

It seems that one way to begin to achieve Goldberg's suggested alteration is to address directly his third point: the refusal to utter racist sentiments. This practice would call into repeated and constant question virtually every single utterance of every single person because the binary logic and hierarchy of thought that produces racist discourse are present in virtually every utterance made in the English language.[9] The binary logic system that undergirds English language usage not only allows for the reproduction of discriminatory divisions made on the basis of race, class, and gender, among others, but insists upon them. The practice of refusing to participate in language uses that produce discrimination would foreground the logic system upon which those discourses rest. It is at this point that the logic system that produces and perpetuates the division of American culture into class and ethnic groups could be reconfigured into a logic system that could accommodate both the first and third fundamental factors Goldberg articulates: an alteration of the class system and a conscious abandonment of racist discourse by means of his second factor, "a transformation and extinction of the formal components of [racial discourse]." A theory of a logic system that functions on a premise of multiplicity would necessarily affect the material practices of the ideological system that it served.

If we understand the ways in which language functions to set up differences and the hierarchies that value those differences, and if we refuse to participate in such discourse, we will not be able to speak. We need a new set of metaphors, new figures of speech, and new ways of making sense out of our lived experiences. Goldberg believes that this "new language" can be achieved. He suggests that through a consideration of his three "fundamental factors" a discourse can be formulated that can be "constructively assumed because it authorizes and articulates acceptable acts, [and does not merely issue] authoritative orders and injunctions [that are] imposed on subjects" (Goldberg, 1990: 314). What Goldberg seems to be proposing is not simply a discourse that stands in opposition to racist discourse, but a rhetorical structure that could support a multiplicity of counterdiscourses. It is a rhetorical structure that can accommodate situatedness, multiple subjectivities, and an awareness of the arbitrariness of meaning. Goldberg's theory can be useful in moving toward communication that will influence a Habermasian "volition." What we teach in the university participates in subsequent systems of "privileged" activity and knowledge. Therefore, if we begin to teach equity in, as well as respect for, difference, that concept will become internalized by other social institutions. Paradoxically, it will also change the "privileged" position of institutions of higher learning.[10] The aim of a critical multiculturalism is to establish the will to make such changes.

Henry Giroux offers cultural studies as a theoretical model that can produce a "basis for creating new forms of knowledge by making language constitutive of the conditions for producing meaning as part of the knowledge/power relationship" (Giroux, 1992: 164). By reconfiguring the ways in which American culture perceives language use, the logic system that supports that language use is brought under scrutiny. An awareness of the relationship between the practice of uttering racist ideas and the reproduction of racism allows a space in which one can interrogate the logic behind such an utterance. This can lead to a reconceptualization of the ways in which knowledge and power are produced. This awareness, Giroux asserts, can only change the ways in which cultural institutions function. Giroux continues to explain that while awareness is a crucial step, practice and active participation in changing the ways in which knowledge and power are constituted must be acted out. It is through both theoretical reconceptualization *and* pedagogical practice that self-reflexively implements a constant critique of the ways in which the language used to construct them as a language usage that "articulates acceptable acts" that we may begin to articulate theories and practices that refuse to function as "the reflex of the logic of domination." In this way, Giroux argues, a rhetoric of multiplicity could be produced (Goldberg, 1990: 314; Giroux, 1992: 165). This pedagogy would serve as "a cultural practice engaged in the production of knowledge, identities, and desire" (Giroux, 1992: 166). This critical pedagogy moves away from an understanding of education as a "transmission of knowledge" to an understanding of education as a process that "engages its own ideological assumptions" (166).

It is through the process of examining the ideological foundations of America's institutions of higher learning that an awareness of the role that language usage plays in the reproduction of that ideology is achieved. Through this awareness comes an understanding of the processes through which knowledge and meaning are produced in the academy, which then allows for an understanding of the power relationships present in knowledge/meaning-making processes. It is at this point that we can consider the economic relationships and motives that drive such ideological processes. By making clear the processes by which knowledge is produced through certain language uses, Giroux suggests that a new knowledge is produced. With this new knowledge we can begin to construct Goldberg's second "fundamental factor," the "transformation of the formal components [of racist discourse], its grammar and language" (Goldberg, 1990: 313). This transformation must necessarily function in relationship with new material practices. These are the practices that a critical multiculturalism aims to produce.

Goldberg's call for the eradication of racist discourse can only bear fruit through a large-scale alteration of the ways in which knowledge is produced, and this means an alteration in the ways in which the institutions charged with producing "privileged" knowledge are understood and situated in relationship to other social and economic institutions. Giroux suggests that these changes can only be made through changes in America's institutions of higher learning. His critical pedagogy "suggests inventing a new language for resituating teacher/student relations within pedagogical practices that open up rather than close down the borders of knowledge and learning" (Giroux, 1992: 166). This is important because a process that resituates a dominant cultural knowledge-making system as one system among many foregrounds the relationship between the institutions that keep the culture functioning. This can lead to an examination of the relationship between cultural economic systems and cultural knowledge institutions. Giroux calls for teachers to:

Provide conditions for students to engage difference not as the proliferation of equal discourses grounded in distinct experiences, but as contingent and relational constructions that produce social forms and identities which must be made problematic and subject to historical and textual analyses. (1992: 175)

I would add that changes made in the student/teacher relationship would also entail changes to be made in the relationship between teacher and administration, between theorist and practitioner, and between the academy and the culture-at-large. Goldberg writes:

A well-defined field of discourse arises out of a *discursive formation*. This consists of a totality of ordered relations and correlations of subjects to each other and to objects; of economic production and reproduction, cultural symbolism and signification; of laws and moral rules; of social, political, economic, or legal inclusion and exclusion. The sociodiscursive formation consists of a range of rules: "is's" and "oughts," "do's" and "don'ts," "cans" and "cannots," "thou shalts" and "thou shalt nots." Conditions of existence, production and reproduction, preservation, transformation and dissolution at a given historical conjuncture define an *object* that can be spoken of. They determine also the *mode* in terms of which the object can be analyzed, its elements named and classified, its functions explained. Rules constitutive of a discursive field are promoted in this elaboration of object and mode. (Goldberg, 1990: 297)

I quote Goldberg at length here because he so vividly describes the intertwined nature of the institutions that founded American culture.

Changes in America's institutions of higher learning must necessarily affect other institutions. The formation of discourse—be it racist, elitist or critically multicultural—cannot avoid implicating all of the institutions of the culture. Goldberg describes the parameters of discourse, and through his focus on these relationships a pattern emerges that illustrates the presence of a rhetorical relationship between all discourse communities in American culture, which can only, qualitatively, produce the same discourse. It stands to reason then that, conversely, if one institution is inherently racist/classist, all institutions are inherently racist/classist. This principle means that institutions of higher learning are racist/classist through their relationship to other institutions that participate in the production of discourse.

Just as Goldberg illustrates that the borders produced by practices of division, hierarchy, and separation become more readily visible as these concepts are repeated, so Giroux's critical pedagogy suggests a perpetual examination of borders between all of the "zones of cultural difference" in order to foreground the relationship between the "creation, sustenance, and formation" of those borders. Giroux's project is to produce a "[c]ritical pedagogy [that] serves to make visible those marginal cultures that have been traditionally suppressed in American schooling" (Giroux, 1992: 170). Just as Goldberg is working for the eradication of a logic system that reproduces racist discourse, Giroux is working for the eradication of an educational system that can only reproduce the borders that support racist/classist discourse. A critical multiculturalism engages both of these theories in order to produce theoretical and practical responses to noncritical multiculturalism. These theories and practices cannot yet effectively examine the border of the dominant culture because it is obfuscated by a theoretical and practical focus on visible racial difference.

The discourse of what is currently referred to as the dominant culture must become one discourse among many, and its borders must be defined before an examination of the relationships that produce and reproduce it can begin. This means that economic difference as well as cultural, gendered, religious, and sexual differences must all be considered as means of marking individuals as members of the dominant culture. This is a critical multicultural practice. A critical multiculturalism can begin to deconstruct and delimit "the dominant culture" and redefine it as merely one cultural model among many. In this way we can begin to change the practices of the cultural institutions in the United States.

Practice is the product of the institution. If the institution is racist or elitist then its practice will reproduce those values. Theories such as

Goldberg's and Giroux's mediate the relationship between practice and the institution that produced it in order to produce theory that can inform practices that reshape the institutions that support them and that they support. Goldberg insists that "resistance must also oppose the *language* of the oppressor" (Goldberg, 1990: 314). Giroux states that through a discourse of opposition, oppression is opposed. These two statements seem to be a perfect binarism, and yet they explode the binary. We do not have to escape the binary in order to produce terms that allow for multiplicity within the terms of the binary.[11] Goldberg seems resistant to accepting any discourse that uses the terms of the binary, and yet, presently there are no others. Giroux has no trouble using the logic system against itself. These are theoretical problems that cannot be solved until practice produces changes in the institutions that will allow us to be able to make "sense" out of such arguments.

Once theorists begin to produce theories that consider the material relationship between their theory and the institution that produces them and it, then teachers can begin to use that theory in order to produce practices that will allow them to negotiate their own relationship between their practices and the institution within which they practice them. When practices are developed that acknowledge the limitations of the institution, and the limitations of those who work within the institution, then theory can be developed that will address that whole new set of problems produced by the shifts that will result in institutional practice. It is dialectic, but not Hegelian dialectic. It is a dialectic that folds back in on itself to change where we are and not one that determines where we will go. Progressive oscillation between practice and theory is a characteristic of critical multiculturalism. The aim of critical multiculturalism is not to erase difference in the speculative future, but to change the ways we think about difference today.

NOTES

1. The term "critical multiculturalism" has been used prior to my usage of it most notably by David Palumbo-Liu, Henry Giroux, Barry Kanpol, and Peter McLaren. However, these theorists were theorizing. The offer of practices that could respond to those theories was limited. It is important that critical multiculturalism consist of both theory and practice working with and against one another in a continuous dialectic. This also forces the theorist to consider, or rather reconsider, the traditional relationship between theorist and practitioner.

This is a relationship that must be reconfigured in any reconceptualization of the function of the university as an institution of American culture.

2. It can be argued here that affirmative action and multicultural curricula have been developed to fight against this kind of racialized hierarchy. However, as a mechanism of an ideology that is based upon a racist philosophy institutions of higher learning can only fulfill the needs of that larger social agenda. It is in this way that public schools and community colleges that offer vocational training are largely attended by people of color, and private schools, which provide primarily liberal arts education and are not bound by law to adhere to affirmative action laws or even offer a multicultural curriculum, are still primarily white. The "lower" level of schooling functions to produce not an elite class of intellectuals but a colored class of workers. In this way the academy has produced a hierarchy within itself in order to produce a hierarchized set of intellectuals, which follows the model of the larger culture.

3. In an essay entitled, "PC, or Do the Right Thing," Berndt Ostendorf writes, "could it be that the new discourse of multiculturalism serves to repress a consideration of the more difficult issue of class that to most Americans seems so un-American"? (Ostendorf, 1993: 212).

4. See Robert Bellah, *Habits of the Heart.*

5. See Henry Louis Gates, Jr.'s introduction to *"Race," Writing and Difference* and Henry Trueba's discussion of race and ethnicity in his essay entitled "Race and Ethnicity: The Role of Universities in Healing Multicultural America."

6. I refer the reader to the affirmative action furor that began in the mid-1990s at the University of California. The regents voted to disband affirmative action criteria in their admissions policy beginning in September 1996. This policy change has now been postponed for one year at the undergraduate level. Some would theorize that President Atkinson requested the postponement because the disbanding of affirmative action cannot happen until we as a culture learn how to value cultural differences that are marked by criteria other than physiological difference. This, one would hope. I theorize that the president postponed the shift in selection criteria because of the administrative and bureaucratic technicalities such as shift could incur.

7. The Office of Management and Budget (that is responsible for producing categories of ethnic identity in this country) has institutionalized this paradigm of ethnic identity through its implementation of quota forms used for purposes of affirmative action. There are no multicultural categories; each individual must choose a unified identity category. A spokesman for the NAACP has argued that the inclusion of a multicultural category would simply drain resources from the groups traditionally recognized as "minority". This sets ethnic groups in opposition to one another in a way that reflects the more traditional white/non-white binary mode of identity in American culture. This set of multiple binaries cannot itself tolerate any identity that does to contain itself within one of the binary categories (Bizjak, 1994: 194).

8. I would like to point up Goldberg's use of the word "counterdiscourses." It seems that we cannot currently function linguistically outside the binary paradigm. On a practical level this is the logic system that "makes sense" for us, and this is why Goldberg appears to be asking for changes that could only be produced by a logic system that does not currently exist.

9. Let me provide an example. I have collected some "figures of speech," that are familiar to any native English speaker or anyone fluent in the English language. Does one "ask questions for clarification or further positioning"?" It is often difficult to discuss one important topic because "there are so many more important issues." Some of these issues cannot logically stand on their own and must be assisted by a speaker who can "lend authority to [the] issue." When someone disagrees with the topic it is appropriate to dismiss it because of the lack of "a responsible reason" to continue. Many things are decided to be "A step above and in your best interest." This usually occurs when the issues were clearly presented by someone was able to state "the value of it [and] and [could take the conversation] in a clear direction." Many of these statements can be immediately understood as qualitative, stratifying, teleological and discriminating. Some are a little more discrete, but with examination one can see that "further positioning" or "more important reasons" imply a hierarchy of thought that is constantly being reinforced and reproduced with every utterance. When these kinds of comments are made in the context of racial distinction they become racist sentiments.

10. This explains the liberal/conservative debate I have outlined in chapter one that attempts to maintain the status quo of the institution through a discussion of radical change. The character of the institution is to preserve itself. This seems to be a symptom of the economic system of capitalism. Market competition drives the desires to not only survive, but to exist in a position of privilege. Once that privileged position is achieved the goal is to maintain it at all costs.

11. In *Gender Trouble: Feminism and the Subversion of Identity*, Judith Butler writes:

The shift from an *epistemological* account of identity to one which locates the problematic within practices of *signification* permits an analysis that takes the epistemological mode as one possible and contingent signifying practice. Further the question of *agency* is reformulated as a question of how signification and resignification work. (Butler, 1990: 144)

3
Critical Multicultural Readings of Four American Texts

American literary history allows for a discussion regarding the ways American literature has functioned as a means of defining the American identity. For the purposes of this argument, American literature consists of texts produced by natural born or naturalized Americans and deemed of literary merit by contemporary critical discourse. This definition foregrounds the national boundaries used to demarcate Americanness. The experiences—no matter how diverse—contained in those American texts are American experiences. This opens up an understanding of American subjectivity as being multiplicitous and diverse. To categorize a text as multicultural maintains its status as marginal by producing it as somehow not American.[1] The dynamic that allows for what appears to be a natural division between American literature and multicultural literature follows the model of intergroup relations in American culture. This dynamic has historically focused on the hierarchization of cultural groups, and has been constructed in terms of visibility and invisibility. "Multicultural" texts have struggled for visibility. However, visibility, as their marginalized status might suggest, does not necessarily equal power. Why then has this trope of visibility/invisibility been embraced culturally as indicating a relationship of power that privileges the visible?

AnnLouise Keating cites Toni Morrison and bell hooks as two theorists who have recently argued for understanding the invisibility of whiteness that shifts the terms of the trope of visibility/invisibility and suggests that the more powerful position is one of invisibility. Keating writes that "A number of theorists have associated 'whiteness' with mystery, absence, and death"(Keating, 1995: 907). This invisibility allows a dominant Anglocentric cultural group to efface the differences that exist within the group by constantly shifting the cultural gaze to the differences present outside of the group. One of the reasons it seems mysterious and implacable might be the presence of untold cultural differences contained within a cultural fable that says there exist no differences between individuals who belong to the dominant culture.

Critical multicultural readings of Mark Twain's *Adventures of Huckleberry Finn* (1884), Ralph Ellison's *Invisible Man* (1947), and Maxine Hong Kingston's novels *Woman Warrior* (1977) and *China Men* (1989) foreground the function of invisibility in an Anglocentric hegemony. A critical multicultural reading of these texts can investigate the relationship between traditionally "visible" and "invisible" identities that have historically been used to value human identities within the context of American culture. In this way a critical multicultural reading of these texts is comparative in that a critical multiculturalism reads for the relationships that support or critique the production of difference. In this reading of these four texts I am reading for the relationships of power as they are constructed in terms of who is visible and who is invisible. I am reading the construction of one identity in comparison with the construction of another identity in each text, and then I am reading the ways in which these constructions are repeated or challenged in each of the texts respectively. This allows me to compare the ways in which the constructions of the relationships and identities I have read change or do not change. This allows me to then mark either the progression of ideas or the imbrication of a logic pattern.

A critical multicultural reading is not the same as "demonstrating the discursive constitution of identities," that is; looking at the ways in which difference is represented (Lye, 1995: 277). This is the primary function of a noncritical multiculturalism. This practice is problematic because when a text is deconstructed in order to focus on the ways in which identities are linguistically constructed we often do so by "homogeni[zing] the dispositions of, and differences in power between, various kinds of discursive formations" (277). Very often the construction of an identity will serve to reinforce the power dynamic that produces it even when it is constructed in ways that suggest its power to subvert that structure. Reading identity comparatively allows for a reading of the ways in which that identity functions in a variety of milieus. This allows for a focus on the differences that demarcate one identity from another, and can allow for a powerful reading of the ways in which power relationships maintain themselves over centuries.[2]

It may seem odd to have Mark Twain's American classic, *Adventures of Huckleberry Finn* included on a list of multicultural texts as a noncritical multiculturalism has constructed that category of authors Twain's Anglocentric identity seems to displace him. However, a critical multicultural literary theory looks not only at the ways in which identity is discursively performed but at the ways in which discourse sets up relationships that support and perpetuate the power dynamics that produce and value such identities. Twain's text is a valuable critical multicultural text because of its attempt to address just these issues in the last one-fifth of the novel. What is also interesting about Twain's text is the way traditional literary criticism has failed to engage this last part of the book. Perhaps this is because the story of Jim's release from the woodshed requires the critical reader to self-reflexively consider the traditional practices within which he or she participates. These practices have historically been racist, elitist, and oppressive, and remain problematic because they function to assign value to a text and rank it in a hierarchy of texts. Even a critical multicultural literary theory will not avoid this same function. However, it is to be hoped that a more self-reflexive approach to this task may, as Twain's text has, call this function into question.

It is not quite the case that canonized texts produce a singular, fixed identity of who an "American" is and who an "American" is not. Many texts problematize this schema. Too often, however, it seems to have been the function of literary criticism to reproduce precisely those aspects of a work that conform to traditional understandings of an American. In this way the canonized text becomes the model not only for identity, but also for relationships between identities. What seems to have happened historically is that in the critic's role of producing the text as fixed, canonized, and therefore privileged, the critic's function becomes effaced. This process naturalizes and reifies the identities performed in the text and the relationships between the identities. In this way the practice of producing theories about the text produce practices that in turn reinforce and reproduce theories of homogeneity, and fixed identity. This process of education also maintains an "invisible" position for the makers of meaning (the critics), that does not easily allow for shifting meanings to be produced in response to a given text. A critical multicultural literary theory, that is, a theoretical perspective that privileges a multiplicity of meaning and refuses to privilege one representation of cultural identity over another, can be used to understand the ways a text is defined as American or multicultural by virtue of its relationship to the invisible power of the dominant culture. It can also illustrate how that dominant culture effaces or makes itself invisible and in order to naturalize its power to make such relegation.

Somewhere around chapter thirty-four, Twain critic Leo Marx marks the beginning of the one-fifth of *Adventures of Huckleberry Finn* that "jeopardizes the significance of the entire novel" (Marx, 1995: 292).

Eric Sundquist has called those chapters that contain Jim's captivity in the woodshed "'the second slavery' of the nadir . . . embedded in Twain's bitter humiliations of Jim in *Adventures of Huckleberry Finn*" (Sundquist, 1993: 232). Many critics simply gloss over the end of the novel because it seems to run contrary to the antiracist aspects of the earlier parts of the novel that the tradition has been able to identify.[3] I suggest that in order to read Jim's release from the woodshed as something other than a story of "Huck ['s acquiescence to] Tom's ludicrous imprisonment and parodic torment of a man already legally free" (232), a critic must consider the reproductive function of criticism. In so doing, a critical multicultural reading of the last one-fifth of the novel allows for an understanding of Jim as the author of a powerful counter-narrative to Anglocentric literary tradition. It is difficult to "see" this reading when using a noncritical approach. Not only are the traditional values still in place, but this value occludes the opportunity to "see" these characters in any other relationship that one that supports the traditional values assigned to them. Jim's text is thereby occluded by Tom's commentary, Huck's response, and the presence of Twain's narrative voice because of the traditional values assigned to each of these identities. Traditional criticism (read noncritical multiculturalism) does not attempt to read past the opportunity to foreground Jim's difference from the "white" characters that contain him. This traps Jim in his traditional, passive, subservient role and reproduces the same identity from which some critics attempt to release him.

Toni Morrison has argued that "given the confines of the story . . . there is no way for Huck to mature into a moral human being *in America* without Jim" (Morrison, 1992: 56). She explains that Jim must be incarcerated in order to recontextualize his inferior position to Tom and Huck in the new social order of the post-Reconstructionist South, and in order to allow Huck to renegotiate his own new social position. I think Morrison is correct in the terms she has set for the relationship between the characters. Huck's identity is contingent upon Jim's identity, and more important, Tom's identity depends upon maintaining a tension between Huck and Jim.

Near the end of Twain's novel Jim is caught and imprisoned in a woodshed at the back of Aunt Sally's family farm. Tom Sawyer shows up just in time to help Huck figure out how to get Jim free. The two boys take a stroll down to the woodshed and discover that there is a boarded window through which Jim can escape once the board is pried loose. An excited Huck says, "Here's the ticket. This hole's big enough for Jim to get through if we wrench off the board" (*HF*, 1995: 204).[4] Tom replies: "I should hope we can find a way that's a little more complicated than *that*, Huck Finn" (*HF*, 204). Thereby the narrative to free Jim, an already freed slave, begins and takes the reader through the myriad of machinations that make up the last section of the book. The schemes to free Jim seem superfluous to the story, but they are (as Morrison suggests) an integral part of Huck's development. The irony of the situation foregrounds the possibility that something else—something extra-textual—is occurring. The possibility this ironic twist presents is that Huck is not the only character undergoing change at this moment in the novel. The development of Huck's identity as an American author is contingent upon the development of Jim's identity as an African-American author.

At the beginning of chapter thirty-five, the reader may wonder why Jim has not dislodged the board from the woodshed himself, and why he is still sitting in a rickety old woodshed while two small boys discuss his future. This passive behavior is not consistent with the characterization of Jim throughout the middle passages of the novel when we see Jim act as an agent in several episodes. It is, however, akin to the characterization of Jim in the opening episodes of the novel when we see Jim perform the role of "clown" or kowtowing servant within white society. There is a huge difference between what seems to be Jim's inactivity in the shed and his performance in the beginning of the novel. Jim has moved from the performance of subservience to the performance of agency as scripted by a dominant culture.

When Huck planned his own escape at the beginning of the story, he quite ingeniously, if not with the flair of Tom Sawyer, killed himself and disappeared. Tom returns to the story to teach Huck the "rules." In other words, Tom returns to the story in chapters thirty-three through thirty-eight in order to introduce Huck—and Jim—to the Eurocentric tradition of the escape narrative. The incorporation of Jim into the process allows Twain's text to illustrate for the reader how the newly freed slave would be assimilated into the dominant culture through his participation in the practices of the narrative traditions of Western culture. Further, by incorporating Jim into the narrative tradition Huck becomes identified as the privileged author because of his relationship to Jim. Huck will sponsor Jim's escape narrative. Tom will critique their work.

The traditional hierarchy of cultural knowledge over lived experience is what allows a reader to value Tom's position over both Huck and Jim's. In order to get out of the woodshed Jim must produce an escape narrative that satisfies Tom's criteria of the traditional formula of an escape narrative, and Huck participates in that process by serving as the mediator between Jim and Tom. This is not an unproblematic set of relationships. However, they are the traditional identities and relationships acted out in American literary history: the privileged author, the marginalized author, and the critic. If the reading of the text stops here it is easy to walk away with a view of Jim as a powerless and invisible voice subject to the whims of Tom's criticism. However, Jim exercises his own agency in these chapters and thereby illustrates the interdependent relationship between the three identities.

Having rejected Huck's straightforward plan of pulling off a board and having Jim climb through the side of the woodshed Tom says to Huck,

Well, if that ain't jus like you, Huck Finn. You *can* get up the infant-schooliest ways of going at a thing. Why, hain't you ever read any books at all? Baron Trenck, nor Cassanova, nor Benvenuto Chelleeny, nor Henri IV, nor none of them heroes? Who ever heard off getting a prisoner loose in such an old-maidy way as that? No; the way all the best authorities does is to saw the bed-leg in two, and leave it just so, and swallow the saw dust, so it can't be found. (*HF*, 209)

We can read in this passage Tom's identity as critic and gatekeeper of the "tradition" as he reminds Huck that the methods they employ in the process of releasing Jim are meaningful only in relationship to certain culturally privileged texts. Tom knows the tradition, Huck can perform the tradition as directed, and Jim is learning the tradition. Tom begins to formulate a *more traditional plan.* At this point in the story literary criticism has traditionally understood Jim to be a passive observer in his own escape. However, Tom makes it clear that the escape cannot happen without Jim's active involvement. More important, Jim himself must record the action. As they formulate their plan Tom says, "Borrow a shirt too."

"What do we want of a shirt, Tom?" asks Huck.
"Want it for Jim to keep a journal on."
"Journal your granny—*Jim* can't write."
"S'pose he *can't* write—he can make marks on the shirt, can't he, if we make him a pen out of an old pewter spoon or a piece of an old iron barrel-hoop?"

Tom assures Huck that "the best authorities uses their own blood" and Huck seems to accept that (*HF*, 224). However, Tom then suggests that when Jim wants to enter public discourse in order to "send any common ordinary mysterious message to let the world know where he's captivated" that he needs to write that message on the bottom of a tin plate. Huck responds by saying, "Jim ain't got no tin plates" (*HF*, 224).

Tom assures Huck that as long as they are "representing a prisoner" it is perfectly acceptable for them to steal some tin plates upon which Jim can write (*HF*, 225). Huck returns to his original argument that Jim cannot write and therefore, "Can't nobody *read* his plates"(225). To which Tom responds:

That ain't got anything to *do* with it, Huck Finn. All *he's* got to do is to write on the plate and throw it out. You don't *have* to be able to read it. Why half the time you can't read anything a prisoner writes on a tin plate, or anywhere else.

To which Huck wonders,

Well, then, what's the sense in wasting the plates?
Why, blame it all, it ain't the *prisoner's* plates.
But it's *somebody's* plates, ain't it (*HF*, 225)?

The idea that Jim has at least two versions of his narrative, one on somebody else's plates and one in blood on a piece of clothing belonging to the family that had enslaved him, is made quite clearly in this exchange between Huck and Tom. Jim is present but invisible at this point. We get no description of Jim as he sits in the woodshed. It seems he must surely be listening to the considerations of how his freedom will be secured. However, Jim's absence in this exchange is equaled by the absence of a narrative structure. It is pure exchange between Huck and Tom. There is no narration; Huck and Tom seem to have lost their own plates. That is the (tem)plate of discourse. This loss of narrative guidance suggests that the owner of Tom and Huck's "plates" is attempting to produce a space within that Jim can be accommodated as well. At this point in the narrative, Jim is becoming a discursive subject.

Tom and Huck decide that Jim can be accommodated within the structure or template of their discourse by having Jim write on "somebody's plates" because Jim must participate. If he has no plates of his own he must write on someone else's but he must write, and he must write a narrative that satisfies the criteria of the traditional formula of the escape narrative. At this point, Tom and Huck begin to refer to Jim as "the prisoner." However, the template of discourse imprisons them all. The only way out of the situation seems to be to renegotiate the traditional structure of discourse that defines meaningful human existence to allow for Jim's participation. Shelley Fisher Fishkin writes that in "1882 Twain wrote his publisher a letter [regarding the *Huckleberry Finn* manuscript that] would be unremarkable were it not for the fact that Twain decided to write it entirely in black dialect"

(Fisher Fishkin, 1993: 103). Twain signs the letter, SL Clemens and then adds a postscript that says, "I wrotened to Cholly Webster' bout dem goddam plates en copyrights". (104). Twain may have included a space in his own letter within which Jim could inquire about the status of his plates. The letter was signed "SL Clemens," indicating a possible conflation of Jim with Clemens, the author. This would indicate that the positions occupied by Jim, the new author, and Clemens, the accepted author, are similar in some ways. The postscript could be read as a continuation of the knowledge that Jim gained in the woodshed that extends from the production of the text within the parameters of the tradition to the means by which that text is produced and disseminated. Following this line of logic the representation of Jim's concern in Clemen's own letter suggests that Twain and Jim are both concerned with the larger cultural forces that affect their texts.

Had the letter not been signed at all one might conclude that Jim himself had written it. In chapter thirty-eight Huck reminds the reader that Jim had argued with Tom by saying he "didn't know how to make letters," and that Tom responded by saying that he would teach him how to write by "blocking them out for him" (*HF*, 1995: 239). This suggests that Tom did teach Jim how to write. Huck's function as narrator of the escape structures what Jim has written, and Jim definitely writes something. This suggests that Jim can be incorporated into the template of the narrative. Jim's first act of participation in his release is to make marks on a tin plate and throw it out the window of the woodshed. Do the plates contain legible marks? We do not know, and this fact foregrounds the interpretive power of Tom. Tom understands and privileges the act of marking the plates and throwing them into the public sphere; which marks Jim makes on the plates does not seem to matter, Tom's knowledge of the tradition will make them meaningful.

Once Jim leaves the woodshed he will have knowledge of the tradition of the "plates." He will have moved to a position wherein he could assert discursive agency. This, however, is not an unproblematic position. The process of "freeing" Jim can be read as a set of practices through which Jim's cultural experience is appropriated. Jim is to make his mark on someone else's plates and hand them over to Tom and Huck. Huck who can produce a narrative, albeit a raw and unrefined narrative, will learn from Tom how to interpret the plates and make Jim's text meaningful in ways that conform to the conventions of traditional escape narrative. In this way Huck becomes the mentor for Jim, and Tom allows them to assimilate into the Western tradition. Huck, because of his "advanced knowledge," is privileged. Jim because of his appearance will be marginally assimilated. This marginalization affords Tom and Huck the maintenance of their privileged positions while they incorporate Jim into the narrative that supports their privileged position. In this way Jim exists to support the privileged positions that Tom and Huck occupy. This is Morrison's argument. This set of practices also serves as a fictional analogue to the historical practices associated with heavily mediated drafts of slave narratives. These narratives were frequently preceded by a preface and followed with an Afterword written by a white "friend of the author." [5] It seems clear that Jim understands that in order to write himself into subjectivity he must do so in a way that can be sanctioned by Tom. He marks on the plate and throws it out the window. However, we may have forgotten that Jim still has the shirt.

Jim's participation required that he mark on the plates and send out "any little common ordinary mysterious message to let the world know where he is captivated" (*HF*, 224). It also required that he keep a journal, written in blood on a shirt stolen off of the clothes line belonging to the white slave-owning family within whose woodshed he has been "captivated." Near the end of the "escape" narrative Tom says that, finally, all Jim needs to do is to scrawl a message and his coat of arms on the wall of the shed before he can escape. Huck and Jim are both perplexed by this suggestion because as Jim says, "I hain't got no coat of arms; I hain't got nuffin but dish-yer ole shirt, en you knows I got to keep the journal on dat" (*HF*, 237). Jim has participated in his own narrative escape, and he has internalized the literary values that allow a Eurocentric culture to value such an escape. However, he has also maintained his own blood-written narrative of the experience. Later in the story Aunt Sally and her family find all of the items that Huck and Tom had imported into the woodshed as props to help Jim understand his escape experience in terms they privileged. One of the items found was the shirt. It is interpreted by all as a sure sign of Jim's mental instability. They are not capable of interpreting the marks on Jim's shirt because while it may be written in marks they understand they cannot "make sense" out of the experience. Jim's shirt is an unmediated experience. We hear no more about the plates. However, Twain's letter to the publisher suggests that Jim's plates had been mediated and sent into the public sphere in a context that a general reader could understand.

Teresa A. Goddu and Craig V. Smith argue that the slave narrator, being "born into an existential vacuum—no name, no family, no birthdate, no rights, no geographical or social heritage [must assert] his position in the world by vocally and textually asserting his status [and, thus, write] the self into being" (Goddu and Smith, 1989: 824-825).

Frederick Douglass, according to Goddu and Smith, "in [his 1845 slave] narrative . . . [shifts] the origin of linguistic power [from] the single voice of the white word [to create a] play between the poles of African and American voices" (823). The authors name this "play of power", a "double-consciousness." It begins as the author's "attempt to imitate the master's original voice [and] ends by creating a ... truly originating Afro-American expressivity" (824). Jim can be read as having written himself into existence through the practice of imitating—or being coerced to imitate—a dominant voice. His blood-written journal can be read as the source from which he may begin to produce a "truly originating Afro-American expressivity." However, Jim also made his marks on the plates appropriated by Tom and Huck. This process may entrap him in a double-consciousness. Jim's struggle may be the constant vacillation between the performance of he who can "imitate the Master's original voice" and, possessing the skills of reproduction, the source of a counter narrative. In this way he will be both invisible, as he is subsumed by the voice of the master, and visible as he takes on the role of the critic of the master narrative.

In the "freeing" of Jim from the woodshed in Twain's text, we can see the manner in which a dominant American discourse assimilated African American subjectivity as one that was different from the dominant subject. Without the presence of Jim's difference Huck cannot assume his position as a privileged author—that is one who is able to interpret Jim's voice in terms of the dominant culture. However, consider the new power dynamic this new relationship offers. The text suggests that not only Jim, but all discursive voices are entrapped by a literary tradition that demands the reproduction of certain relationships of power. This means that if Jim is read as invisible and disempowered then all authors are invisible and disempowered until and unless they achieve critical value, this does not disallow Jim's agency. It constructs Jim as an American author learning how to master the conventions that will gain him critical acceptance. This is a shift from reading Jim as powerless and subservient to a reading of Jim as an American author who is gaining a discursive presence. The escape narrative cannot be constructed without Jim's marks on the plate. Huck cannot privilege himself as an American author, and Tom cannot assert his value as gatekeeper and critic without Jim, but this does not render Jim powerless.

We cannot see Jim during his imprisonment in the woodshed. Jim's invisibility seems to foreshadow Ellison's *Invisible Man* who, upon accepting his own invisibility, became "un-named(ly)" powerfully. Jim's invisible presence in the woodshed allows him access to the means by which he can begin to write his own narrative of power relationships. It is for this reason that Huck and Tom allow the townspeople to chain Jim up so tightly following his release from the woodshed. Twain seems to be suggesting that Jim is more dangerous to the dominant narrative following his participation in the construction of his narrative.

Jim's physiological difference appears to be the justification for having him in the shed; however, it is his (invisible) cultural difference that (does not justify but) explains the boys' treatment of Jim in effecting his release from the shed. Jim's physical presence may be effaced during the process of writing himself into the narrative of American literary history because his physiological difference must be conflated with cultural difference. During the time we cannot "see" Jim his cultural experiences—his African experiences—are appropriated. Discursively, culturally and physically he becomes "the prisoner"(*HF*, 225). This imbricates his cultural differences into his physiological difference and naturalizes his cultural difference so that we immediately and unthinkingly recognize his cultural difference because of the way he looks. When Jim emerges from the woodshed he is an American with a difference. He is an African American, and because of the process through which his life experience was appropriated by the Eurocentric tradition it seems he is to be forever marked. The African American, in Twain's text, is the voice that must be interpreted by those white, male Americans who understand the traditions that make voices meaningful. This hierarchization of cultural knowledge over cultural experience allows for the construction of Huck as white, male, and normatively American and Jim as the non-normative American. In Twain's text, the construction of these identities and the relationship that result is, at the very moment it is performed, effaced.

Tom breaks off his explanation of why Jim must mark on the plates at the "breakfashorn," because to continue to explain the process through which Jim will write himself into the tradition of Eurocentric captive narratives would have been to articulate the process of appropriation and assimilation. By breaking off the conversation at the "breakfashorn" Twain can return to the narrative of escape without commenting upon it. The series of maneuvers the three characters go through in order to get Jim out of the woodshed become naturalized through the act of omitting critical comment upon them. Jim's discourse allows him to represent himself as a prisoner in terms that Tom understands and privileges. In this way Jim becomes a visible, different American imprisoned in a literary tradition that requires his mark of difference in order to perpetuate itself, while Twain makes invisible the process by which that transformation occurred.

Jim is more powerful when he is invisible, for without his visible presence Huck cannot maintain his position as that author who is able to interpret and interpellate his work in terms of the dominant culture. One waits and wonders when Jim will get tired of fooling around with the boys and simply break out of the woodshed. One wonders what Jim has written on the journal shirt. This quality of not knowing what to expect of Jim places him in a powerful position. Even after Jim is shown to have decided to participate in the production of his escape narrative and to conform to the conventions, he remains powerful because he now has access to the cultural knowledge that can allow him to rewrite the narrative at any moment. Jim follows a program of assimilation that holds the promise that he will eventually be allowed to tell his own tale. This is the history of American literature.

Toni Morrison writes "It is important to see how inextricable Africanism is or ought to be from the deliberations of literary criticism and the wanton, elaborate strategies undertaken to erase its presence from view" (Morrison, 1992: 8-9). American literary criticism reproduces a Eurocentric aesthetic as the standard of literary excellence by marking that which is not quite American. Africanism is both that which is not American and that which is made into Americanism. In this way Africanism cannot be erased because it must be present and visible in order to function as that which is not American. It is the way in which the presence of Africanism is valued that is problematic.

The American tradition set itself outside the British tradition by producing a difference that was unique to it. Morrison argues that "blackness" has been used as a silent presence to define "literary whiteness." I would open up that argument to suggest that "redness" and "yellowness" have also historically played similar silent roles.[6] The "multicultural" author is different not only or primarily because of his or her physiological difference, but because he or she has been culturally constructed as one whose cultural experience is "O"ther than the experiences of a traditional, white, male author from the earliest moments of his or her experiences. Physiological difference is conflated with cultural difference, and because of the conflation and the effacement of the construction of the multicultural American as not "of the dominant culture," the literary work of those authors is received as an expression of innate difference and not cultural difference. This is not to efface the very real differences experienced by authors of multicultural texts, or to assert that the work produced by such authors is not very different in content. It is to assert that the practices of accommodation, appropriation, and assimilation—noncritical multiculturalism—construct what looks like immutable difference whose value can never change. This immutable quality threatens to forever bind multicultural authors in a double-consciousness.

Morrison suggests that it is not only the literary work done by white American authors that can be read for the ways "European sources for cultural hegemony were dispersed [and] the process of organizing American coherence through a distancing of Africanism became the operative mode of a new cultural hegemony" (8). We can read this construction and simultaneous effacement of difference in the critical work of American critics of all ethnic backgrounds, and works written by authors representative of other racially marked groups of Americans as well. We can read the reproduction of Eurocentric value in the work of anyone who is attempting to be assimilated into that tradition; or, anyone who unquestioningly or even questioningly values that tradition. The Eurocentric aesthetic is the measuring stick by which all producers of knowledge in American culture have been judged. However, it is not by simply making the production or reproduction of a subordinate identity visible as different or by making visible the identity in relief of the white, male icons of American literature that the privileged position of a Eurocentric aesthetic is perpetuated. It is by making the practices that produce and reproduce the relationships between those identities invisible that a dominant culture maintains its position of power.

Twain implies the power inherent in invisibility for the African American author, and Ralph Ellison makes this invisibility his theme. Indeed, the trope of invisibility in American literature belongs to Ralph Ellison. Ellison's 1981 introduction to his novel, *Invisible Man*, opens with the question, "What if anything is there that a novelist can say about his own work that wouldn't be better left to the critics" (*IM*, vii)?[7] His argument seems to be that the author as the producer of the work is perhaps too close to the process of production to be able to meaningfully critique his own work. The sentiment that underlies both the comment and the argument is, however, that the critic's function is to make the work of the author meaningful.[8] This argument alludes to the framework of tradition that the critic represents. Ellison's reference to it, however, makes the tradition that the critic represents visible, and in this way contains the power of the critic.

Ellison constructs an author as one who produces a text and a critic as one who makes it meaningful. The relationship depends upon the ability to maintain the invisible power of the critic, and this depends upon maintaining a belief that invisibility equals powerlessness. Invisibility, in these terms, means occupying an identity that has little social relevance or ability to influence social order. In *Adventures of Huckleberry Finn* it is the appearance of Jim's acceptance of a seemingly apolitical literary aesthetic that produces Tom's and Huck's power. They are invisible voices to Jim as he sits in the woodshed. And yet, they have not been critically interpreted as powerless, but as holding the ability to free him. Likewise Jim is invisible to Huck and Tom as he sits in the woodshed. Once he learns the tradition of the plates, and participates in it he holds the potential power to function as a critic himself.

bell hooks writes that white people can "live as though black people are invisible, and they can imagine they are also invisible to blacks"(hooks, 1992: 168). It would appear that the trope of invisibility is a clear move to oppress the subjectivity of "black folk" and perpetuate a privileged position for "white folk." However, hooks's statement illustrates the double bind of invisibility that the Invisible Man learns at the end of the novel. The control of "the black gaze" in a "white supremacist society" that can "imagine itself invisible to black people" is crucial. (168). The gaze must be controlled because the trope of visibility and invisibility in and of itself is so fragile. It is not a concept that functions in terms of absence or presence but in terms of silence. The "invisible" are understood as critically silent. Hooks writes that "[B]lack folks" were compelled "to assume the mantle of invisibility" in that they could not contribute African discourse to the narrative of American subjectivity. At the same moment, their visibility was required to reinforce their visible difference from "white folks." The assumption of a mantle of invisibility and the control of the black gaze suggests that the white culture could not imagine themselves invisible to "black folks." It suggests that the Anglocentric logic system that named them as the "New Jerusalem" required practices that would constantly reinforce that imaginary existence. The double bind is that imagining itself as invisible allowed the white culture to imagine itself as powerful and conversely imagining "black folks" as invisible render them powerless. Logically this folds in on itself and can only collapse.

As hooks's essay chronicles, "black folks" began to amass vast stores of knowledge regarding the oppressor culture, and they have used that knowledge critically. The mantle of invisibility did not render "black folks" powerless and the invisibility that "white folks" imagined did not maintain their unquestioned position of power. This quagmire of a trope is where a noncritical multiculturalism gets bogged down. Making the "invisible" visible is not a solution because humans are not invisible. Traditions are invisible, culture, in many ways, is invisible, and relationships of power are traditionally invisible. Making those relationships visible is the work of a critical multiculturalism. Mapping out these relationships in terms of African American and Anglocentric culture in America of the middle twentieth century is the valuable work done by Ralph Ellison. He lifts the mantle of invisibility not from the humans traditionally characterized as invisible, but from those who imagined them invisible.[9]

Ellison's *Invisible Man* begins with the story of the Battle Royale that occurred in the protagonist's "pre-invisible days" (*IM,* 18). The pre-Invisible Man as a young boy struggles to present his work to Mr. Colcord, the owner of the "chain of movie houses" and the "bankers, lawyers, judges, doctors, fire chiefs, teachers, [and] merchants"(*IM,* 18). Ellison's listing of the discrete identities of the white audience members does two things. It reinforces the presence of the white hegemony by detailing the power positions occupied by all of the white men. It also foregrounds the differences between them. What unifies these disparate white men is not made visible to the pre-Invisible Man. In fact the pre-invisible young man struggles to see them through the blindfold, or the sweat, or the blood throughout much of the story. In this way these white men can be viewed as invisible, and through the power of the invisible tradition they represent, they serve, unquestioned, as critics of the author's work. The catalog of identities suggests that Ellison is exercising what hooks calls a " 'special' knowledge of whiteness gleaned from close scrutiny of white people"(hooks, 1992: 165). While this list does not give away any of the more subtle differences that may exist among the men, it does indicate an awareness of the differences of class, at the very least, that exist within the otherwise homogeneous appearance of the group that make each individual in the group visible.

The pre-Invisible Man does not yet understand his own participation in the Battle Royale. Therefore, he does not understand the power his future invisibility will afford him because without his presence as that which is not the valorized tradition, there can be no valorized tradition. It is his material—visible—difference and the visible display of his powerlessness that allow the white critics to exercise invisible acts of critique upon him, and thereby imagine themselves as powerful. Unfortunately, at this point in the novel it is the only "visible" role available to him.

Ellison's pre-Invisible Man is interpellated by the white, male crowd and is subjected to critical review when the author stumbles on his own words and replaces the word responsibility with the word equality (*IM*, 31). Ellison provides no narrative explanation of why the pre invisible man would make such a verbal slip. However, the absence of narration that renders the actions of the speaker clearly meaningful illustrates the way in which invisible power to make meaning is exercised by the white audience upon the visible and verbal presence of difference. When it seems that his words reflect a critical response to the world around him he is abruptly sanctioned. It is made clear to the reader, if not to the pre-Invisible Man that he is a writer of value only when his words mimic the noncritical sentiments of the dominant culture. Ellison writes:

The laughter hung smokelike in the sudden stillness . . . . Sounds of displeasure filled the room . . . . But I did not understand . . . .
"say that slowly, son!"
"What, sir?"
"What you just said!"
"Social responsibility, sir," I said.
"You weren't being smart, were you boy?" he said, not unkindly.
"No, sir?"
"You sure that about 'equality' was a mistake?"
"Oh, yes sir," I said. " I was swallowing blood." (*IM*, 31)

Up to this point in the speech the speaker thought the crowd was ignoring him. They were not. They were monitoring him. For, when he uttered a sentiment that ran counter to the values of the dominant culture he was hailed back into place, and because he believed he could be visible and valued by the tradition the white critics possess he stepped back into place. The speaker's desire to be accepted by those tradition forces him to accept and maintain his visibly "O"ther position. However, while he maintains his visibility he cannot critique that tradition. He is to repeat the values of the dominant tradition in the words found acceptable by that tradition and in that way reify the tradition and the role of those who have defined themselves as the purveyors of it. He maintains this position, perhaps, because at this pre invisible stage of his life he believes that to be silent is to be invisible and to be invisible is to be powerless.

The text continues,

I was afraid. I wanted to leave but I wanted also to speak and I was afraid they'd snatch me down. "Thank you, sir," I said, beginning where I had left off and having them ignore me as before. (*IM*, 31)

The author/speaker wants to be a part of this mysterious, violent, and powerful community, but he cannot see (clearly) what it is he desires. As bell hooks writes:

Now many black people live in the "bush of ghosts" and do not know themselves separate from whiteness. They do not know this thing we call "difference." Systems of domination, imperialism, colonialism, and racism actively coerce black folks to internalize negative perceptions of blackness, to be self-hating.... This contradictory longing to possess the reality of the other, even though that reality is one that wounds and negates, is expressive of the desire to understand the mystery, to know through imitation, as though such knowing worn like an amulet, a mask, will ward away the evil, the terror. (hooks, 1992: 166)

The pre-Invisible Man desires the power that the invisible white men possess even though it requires him to internalize the whole tradition of racism and thereby insist upon his own self-loathing. He does not know this of course. However, he understands that the invisibility holds a power of some kind. Once the protagonist relinquishes his desire to be accepted by the invisible force, he himself becomes invisible. Later in the novel Ellison writes:

Here I thought they accepted me because they felt that color made no difference, when in reality it made no difference because they didn't see either color or men .... I had switched from the arrogant absurdity of Norton and Emerson to that of Jack and the Brotherhood, and it all came out the same except now I recognized my invisibility .... So I'd accept it, I'd explore it, rine and heart. I'd plunge into it with both feet and they'd gag .... I didn't know what my grandfather had meant, but I was ready to test his advice .... Let them gag on what they refused to see. Let them joke on it .... (*IM*, 508-509)

Once the protagonist steps out of his role as the visible cultural "O"ther, against which a dominant culture defines itself, he can begin his critique of those cultural practices. Now that he has foregone his attempts to participate in the material role assigned him by the dominant culture, he can see the tradition clearly enough to begin to evaluate, analyze, and critique it. This is the power of invisibility. In becoming aware of the powerful aspects of invisibility, Ellison's Invisible Man finds a space in which he can textually and materially reinvent himself. It is from this space that the famous final words of the novel are offered. The Invisible Man says, "Who knows but that, on the lower frequencies, I speak for you" (*IM*, 581)? Invisibility gained through a refusal to maintain a position as a visible marker of difference that reifies an oppressive tradition allows the Invisible Man to find the power of his voice in the undefined spaces of the underground. Because he is no longer a representative member of this or that social organization, he can now conceive of himself a spokesperson. At this point it is unclear what the Invisible Man will become a spokesman for or against. However, the possibilities offer a myriad of opportunities for the exercise of power.

In his essay, "Spokesman for Invisibility," Thomas R. Whitaker writes,

> Must we decide, then, whether our spokesman is an absence, a metaphor for chaos, an antihero caught between death and insurrection, an agent of responsible freedom who has now defined himself, an emergent author in control of the imagination, an Emersonian transparent eyeball, or a black man whose identity is rooted in vernacular tradition? Perhaps not. Such diverse readings suggest an indeterminacy or plurality of meaning in the book itself. The protagonist may be all of these things, and more besides, in ways that we have yet to explore. (Whitaker, 1987: 388-389)

As Whitaker points up, we need not "decide" what the Invisible Man has become, but we must certainly now engage him on myriad levels. He is no longer a marginalized figure that can be used to define a central figure, he is a series of conflicting and integrally linked characteristics that commonly construct a human psyche. He is no longer easily definable and therefore he must be critically engaged. Finally, he has shifted from being the gazed upon to one who can direct his own gaze, irrepressible, in any direction he chooses. In this way he can become the speaker and not the spoken for; he can become the critic of the tradition that had sought to control his gaze and his voice for generations.[10]

Ellison's Invisible Man has come to understand that through his own narrative he can produce a narrative of African American identity that exists in another (and not an[o]ther) kind of relationship to Eurocentric culture. Ellison problematizes the nature of invisibility. If a multicultural writer accepts invisibility as a powerless position, he or she will be powerless. If the author understands that the terms within which his or her invisibility is defined as powerless is a cultural construct that functions to promulgate that exact belief, he or she may be able to embrace that invisibility within those terms. In this way the author assumes power through the "mantle of invisibility." This is the joke that goes back to George Washington Cable's discussions of miscegenation.[11] African Americans can find power in invisibility, whether that be through passing as a white American or through a disregard for the white cultural myth that tells him or her that he or she is invisible and powerless. Toni Morrison writes,

> One likely reason for the paucity of critical material . . . in matters of race, [is that] silence and evasion have historically ruled literary discourse. Evasion has fostered another substitute language in which issues are encoded, foreclosing open debate. (Morrison, 1992: 9)

Morrison's argument is that this silence reinforces the textually invisible position of the "O"ther and the textual visibility of the dominant culture. I would add, it makes invisible the source of the power that the dominant culture holds and thus mystifies the power of invisibility. As critical practice, this process reproduces the concept that invisibility equals powerlessness and precludes the opportunity to enrich the myth-making systems that currently define positions of visible power. As we move through the twentieth century away from Twain's text we can see a shift away from discussing differences in a "substitute" language. Ellison's text, a traditional multicultural text, engages the issues of difference and invisibility straightforwardly in term of race and social position. Maxine Hong Kingston's texts, *The Woman Warrior: A Memoir of a Childhood Spent Among Ghosts* and *China Men* foreground another aspect of difference that has been understood in terms of invisibility by Eurocentric tradition. Difference is not only marked by what many call "race," it is also marked by gendered identities that need to be examined both independent of and firmly grounded within their "racial" contextualizations.[12]

Kingston initially wrote her two books as one story and then decided to separate them.[13] The separation of the two texts results in stories that are substantially independent and yet textually entwined with one another.[14] The story of *The Woman Warrior* focuses on the many stories told by the narrator's mother who "talk-stories" about her life in China before she was joined with her sojourner husband in America. *China Men* focuses on the ways in which the narrator sets about constructing a family history by tracing the paths of her (multiplicitous) male predecessors. When these narratives are read in tandem they speak to each other. When one text is privileged over another, part of the story is lost. Traditionally, when one text is privileged over another, one is made visible, and one is made invisible. This invisibility impairs the quality of meaning one can then find in the "visible" text.

Kingston has said that, "women's stories have a convolution and the men's stories have more of a linear passage through time. [This is because] those men were making history, while the women were caught up in the old myths" (Geok-Lin Lim, 5). While this comment is problematically essentialist, it sets up a series of dualities: history and myth; male and female; linearity and circularity that need to be considered as both dualities and as individual component parts of a duality. Kingston's texts are complex because she constructs not only Chinese American identity, but gendered, Chinese, American identity.

When we read the stories in tandem we can see that the Chinese immigrants characterized in the stories respond to the processes of immigration, assimilation, and interpellation they experienced in ways that are clearly gendered. The world inhabited by the "China Men" is one that is full of "demons." The women in the story of the *Woman Warrior* experience the invisible power of dominant cultures—American and Chinese—in the form of "ghosts."

In *China Men*, the narrator tells us "the demons did not treat people of any other race the way they did Chinese"(*CM*, 55). [15] The demons are "capricious"; they invent games (*CM*, 139), and "[only] listen to [other] Demons (*CM*, 144). Demons are dangerous. When the "Driving Out" began, the demons in Denver, Tacoma, and Wyoming all participated in killing and shipping away all the "Chinamen" they could find (*CM*, 148-149). The term "demon" in *China Men* is used to describe types of people who are not only in positions of power but whose power emanates from an uncertain source.[16] The adjectives used to describe the demons foreground that they are not necessarily American, white or male. A demon exists in a position of invisible power against which a subject struggles for agency. In *China Men* we see the struggle occur in the sugar cane fields of Polynesian Hawaii and on the railroads of North America. In *China Men*, men see demons everywhere, whereas women encounter ghosts. The use of the word "Ghost" in *China Men* occurs only once with the arrival in America of MaMa. Looking for the "East Broadway station" the narrator tells us "[MaMa] went from white ghost to white ghost shouting over the trains"(*CM*, 71).

In *The Woman Warrior* the narrator tells us "America has been full of machines and ghosts - taxi ghosts, bus ghosts, police ghosts, fire ghosts, meter reader ghosts, tree trimming ghosts, five and dime ghosts. Once upon a time the world was thick with ghosts" (*WW*, 113).[17] What is also interesting in the above quoted passage is that "America *has been full of machines and ghosts*" (*WW*, 113, my emphasis). The implication seems to be that once mastery is gained over either a ghost or a machine, the power of the thing is lost, and they then become simply what they are. Demons in *China Men function* the same way ghosts *function* in *The Woman Warrior.* Both demon and ghost are unfamiliar, strange and powerful because of their mysterious practices that are mysterious primarily because of the lack of cultural knowledge of those who perceive them. They both instill fear and function to dissuade participation in their practices. However, It is both the manifestation of invisible power that is different for the men and women in these stories and relationships to that power that develop. MaMa engages her ghost as a matter of course. She could either be beaten by her fear of the ghost or battle the ghost. Once battled a ghost tends to disappear. The demons engaged by the men in *China Men* are deadly, and they never seem to go away.

Demons in *China Men* are virtually unreadable and malicious figures much like the ghost MaMa engaged at the To Keung School of Midwifery in Canton. The ghost that MaMa battles in Canton is a sitting ghost "so low in its level of incarnation it did not have the shape of a recognizable animal" (*WW*, 85). However, there are many forms of ghosts in China just as there are many forms of demons in America. What MaMa sees as a ghost, something amorphous that can take many different shapes, and what the male characters see in the form of demons are both entities of power. As MaMa's battle with the ghost in Canton reveals one must battle the ghost knowing that part of its power is one's fear of it (*WW*, 81-85). bell hooks writes,

Black people, especially those living during the historical period of racial apartheid and legal segregation, have similarly maintained steadfast and ongoing curiosity about the "ghosts," "the barbarians," these strange apparitions they were forced to serve. (hooks, 1992: 165)

She uses the same language that Kingston uses to describe the mysterious forces that controlled the world inhabited by Chinese migrants and immigrants. Kingston also uses this language to describe power in China as well. This is not to shift the critical gaze from American culture to Chinese culture, but rather it is to suggest that mysterious political power has been articulated through the use of the metaphor of (in)visibility. This suggests that the trope of visibility is a rhetorical strategy that can be used by a political structure to protect political power. This would suggest that while previously marginalized authors may become "visible" in the publishing arena through the use of their voices, they may not necessarily become powerful. The lesson of invisibility that Kingston's texts teach is the power it holds, and that invisibility does not equal powerlessness.

The lesson learned by the Invisible Man was that even with a full mastery of the secrets of the mysterious power of the white critic he had no place to exist. We see him living in the underground because he has not yet been able to make a space for himself that allows him to exist in a new relationship to that power structure. However, the novel holds the promise that he will develop a powerful new relationship with that political structure through his invisibility. Jim's invisible production of textual reality in the woodshed, juxtaposed with the simultaneous invisibility of Huck and Tom (invisible to Jim) as constraining forces acting upon his production of the text also suggest the power of invisibility. Kingston's novels suggest that invisibility is a powerful weapon. It is a power that is not only perceived by the cultural "O"ther, as Twain's depiction of the woodshed experience suggests, and it is a power that may be perceived differently by different people in different life situations.

Kingston's description of ghosts and demons allows an alternative to understanding difference only in terms of "race" and culture. There are gendered responses to the invisible nature of power that must also be given close examination. As LeiLani Nishime writes in "Engendering Genre: Gender and Nationalism in *China Men* and *Woman Warrior*":

The two books explore different boundaries between myth and history and the public and the private, highlighting the difficulty of finding an identity that encompasses both nation and gender. [Kingston's] manipulation of generic forms opens up a space for her to explore Chinese-American identity and to imagine the different shapes it can take. (Nishime, 1995: 81) [18]

A critical multicultural approach to reading and valuing works produced by American authors can allow for a consideration of the myriad ways in which human subjects exist in relationship with one another. It allows for multiple positions of power and foregrounds the social constructedness of the relationship between what we traditionally identify as the empowered and the disempowered. That is not to say that recognition of the socially constructed nature of these relationships will end them on a cultural level. However, mapping out the ways in which myriad positions of power become imbricated in the binary relationship of empowered/disempowered can allow for the development of critical multicultural practices that will bring these mechanisms of social control into question.

NOTES

1. This also opens up the problem of effacement. How, in making a multicultural text American do I efface the valuable differences these texts contain? This leads to the next question for all literary critics, and that is how do I mark that value without effacing its difference and in such a way that I allow it to stand as representative of American culture?

2. The quoted material is taken from Colleen Lye's brilliant essay entitled: "*M. Butterfly* and the Rhetoric of Anti-essentialism." In her essay Lye discusses the performance of D. H. Hwang's play in Singapore. It is through a cross-cultural reading of the play that we can see the geo-political implications

of the work that American feminist critics have missed because of their focus on a reading of gendered roles in the play. Lye's argument is that a focus on gender in the play "keeps the binary terms of East/West and female/male in place, and that actually renders invisible the structure of power that constitutes them" (1995: 276). Lye argues that Hwang's play, even through the machinations of shifting gender and desire, maintains the same power roles that the play appears to critique, and that his practice of shifting and mystifying the gender identification of the characters allows him to make invisible the processes that set up the power relationships between East/West, female/male.

3. For an impressive catalogue of these interpretations see Shelly Fisher Fishkin's *Was Huck Black,* and also the 1995 annotated edition of *Adventures of Huckleberry Finn* edited by Gerald Graff and James Phelan.

4. All references to Mark Twain's *Adventures of Huckleberry Finn* are taken from Boston: Bedford, 1995 edition, Gerald Graff and James Phelan eds, hereafter cited as *HF*.

5. A look at the narratives in Henry Louis Gates, Jr.'s *Classic Slave Narratives* supplies evidence for the mediation of the "voice" of the author by a white mentor.

6. One need only return to the earliest days of the emerging body of what is now defined as American literature to see the ways in which the "evil native" presence was used to shore up the definitive quality of the positive white presence on the continent. I refer the reader to Mary Rowlandson's "The Narrative of the Captivity and Restoration of Mrs. Mary Rowlandson."

7. All references to Ralph Ellison's *Invisible Man* are taken from Random House, vintage books, 1989 edition, hereafter cited as *IM*.

8. Ellison's concern for and interest in literary, aesthetic tradition is foreground by Kimberly W. Benston in the introduction to her collection of critical essays, *Speaking For You: the Vision of Ralph Ellison,* gathered together in order to "reflect the dynamic *interplay* of aesthetic practice and cultural perception that [is] the cornerstone of Ellison's vision" (1987: 8).

9. To understand invisibility as power would empower the invisible man and allow the invisible man the same privilege that the invisible tradition maintains. Critic Tang Soo Ping tries to empower Ellison's invisibility, however, the approach taken only serves to further reinforce the traditional understanding of visibility and invisibility as diametrically opposed forces that can only be understood in terms of power and powerlessness, respectively. In an essay titled, "Ralph Ellison and K.S. Maniam: Ethnicity in America and Malaysia, Two Kinds of Invisibility," Ping writes:

Ellison convincingly depicts the richness and beauty of Negro culture and tradition in the United States . . . . More significantly, he establishes the essential place of Black culture in American society . . . . Invisibility, instead of just representing the deprivation and dispossession of a minority group, also evokes, in contrast, a growing sense of cross-cultural ties, and ultimately identifies the situation of modern man, isolated and alone, but not without the potential to be and to act. (Ping, 1993-1994: 82)

Ping follows the formula of criticism that privileges that which stands outside of tradition for its position as just that. The invisibility of a deprived and dispossessed group eventually works to more clearly define the position of "modern man" a literary era produced for and about White Males who were neither deprived nor dispossessed in the very material ways in which the African American subject was.

The struggle for material "visibility" on the part of the African American author highlights the existential struggle of "modern man" and thereby is once again relegated to the role of defining that which is not "modern man" and thereby subject to none of the same existential angst suffered by those who possess the ability to shift from material dispossession to existential dispossession. Ping reinforces the concept that visibility is contingent upon recognition within a specific historic, socioeconomic tradition.

10. In his essay, "To Move without Moving: An Analysis of Creativity and Commerce in Ralph Ellison's Trueblood Episode," Houston A. Baker quotes Ellison as having written "Life is as the sea, art a ship in which man conquers life's crushing formlessness" (Bentson, 1987: 322). Ellison's Invisible Man in a sense jumps that ship. We cannot "see" him at the end of the novel because we do not know how to see him. He has discarded the form of the spoken for and is moving toward the form of he who speaks for others. However, at the end of the novel we do not know what that form looks like.

11. Eric Sundquist discusses this idea briefly in chapter three of *To Wake the Nations: Race in the Making of American Literature*. Cable's point was that miscegenation was not a danger posed by dark-skinned blacks, but by light skinned blacks. Those "invisible" African Americans could more easily integrate into "white" culture without detection and thereby "overcome" the dominant culture. That is the joke. Invisibility is the power possessed by African Americans (Sundquist, 250).

12. Shirley Geok-Lin Lim is the editor of a collection of essays entitled, *Approaches to Teaching Kingston's "The Woman Warrior."* In the introduction to this work she writes that "a number of studies focus on *The Woman Warrior* and *China Men* as a paired opus" (Geok-Lin Lim, 1991: 15). She goes on to list the various studies that look at these works either singly or in tandem in terms of gendered identity.

13. In an interview with Paula Rabinowitz, Kingston is quoted as having said, "at one time, *The Woman Warrior* and *China Men* were supposed to be one book. I had conceived of one huge book" (Geok-Lin Lim, 1991: 5).

14. This brings to mind Henry Louis Gates, Jr.'s concept of "Speakerly texts" that he discusses at length in his book *The Signifying Monkey* (1988).

15. All references to Maxine Hong Kingston's *China Men* come from Random House, Vintage Books, 1989 edition, hereafter cited as *CM*.

16. In the rest of the story those people who are somehow "O"ther than Chinese are referred to as demons, and all of these occurrences can be found in the narration of the male characters' stories. The "immigration Demon" (*CM*, 55) was encountered by BaBa on his immigration to the "Gold Mountain" a

mythological and strange place. The guardian of such a place it is reasonable to assume would be just as unknowable and strange. The "white demons" (*CM*, 58) encountered throughout the book are first introduced to us as those figures who take BaBa's straw hat off his head on a New York street and smash it for no apparent reason, again strange and indeterminate behavior. The "British demons" (*CM*, 92), "Jesus demons" (*CM*, 92), "Jesus demonesses" (*CM*, 112), "demon convert China Men" (*CM*, 113) are encountered in the tale of "Great Grandfather of the Sandalwood Mountains." This is the tale of Chinese sugar cane plantation workers on Hawaii. The Chinese workers were not even certain of the chores that they were being paid to perform and learned them only through negative reinforcement. That is, they only learned what they were not supposed to be doing when they were lashed or docked on their pay by the demons. Again an unknown and strange relationship. "Black demons, [and] railroad demons"(*CM*, 139), can be found in the chapter on "the Grand Father of The Sierra Nevada Mountains." The white demons would set up different kinds of games in order to get the railroad workers to compete against one another and thereby accomplish the work more quickly. This is a clear description of a seemingly capricious kind of behavior that the China Men are forced to engage in, just as the ghost that MaMa fought forced her to engage in a set of behaviors that only had meaning within the context of one fighting a ghost. "Pig-catcher demons" (*CM*, 140),"miner demons, [and] the demons of Tacoma" (*CM*, 148), all demand what would be considered unreasonable behavior in any other situation. "A human body can't work like that." "The demons don't believe this is a human body." The Chinese workers assert, "this is a Chinaman's body" (*CM*, 140). However, the demons could not understand or did not care that their demands were unreasonable, or that their body of knowledge was evidently different than that of the Chinaman's.

17. All references to Maxine Hong Kingston's, *The Woman Warrior: Memoirs of a Childhood Among Ghosts* are taken from Random House, Vintage Books, 1977 edition, hereafter cited as *WW*.

18. Nishime writes an incredibly useful essay on the relationship between ethnic identity and gender identification. She also addresses with great care the history of the generic debates that surround Kingston's two novels.

4
Critical Multicultural Pedagogy

Teaching critical multiculturalism offers an opportunity to move away from fixed patterns of subjectivity and in so doing offers an opportunity to move away from traditional relationships between subjects. It is an opportunity to learn how difference is valued, produced, and reproduced textually as well as materially. The act of naming a classroom "multicultural," in a critical sense, is an act of marking a classroom as a space that will interrogate the differences that exist within it. This is a difficult and much maligned project. However, the critically multicultural classroom allows students to learn how to investigate differences that exist within themselves. In this way the student who has participated in a critically multicultural pedagogy understands that difference is integral to human identity. This produces a student who is less likely to resist difference or to respond to differences perceived outside of him or herself in a negative manner. It also teaches a student to interrogate him or herself, and in this manner, it teaches the student how to interrogate the world in which he or she exists. These are crucial skills in a college classroom, or in a factory, or in a boardroom, or in a household.

In an essay written for *Harpers* author, Mark Edmundson writes, "multiculturalism can be attractive as a well-deployed theory. What could be more valuable than encountering the best work of far flung cultures?" (Edmundson, 1997: 47) In the context of his essay regarding the consumerist environment that the university has become this is a quizzically interesting comment. Not only does his comment reinforce widespread practice of conflating multiculturalism with globalism, but he misses a golden opportunity to proffer a response to the consumerism he sees as controlling the quality of life in institutions of higher education. Critical multiculturalism is concerned with an investigation of difference within the boundaries of a given cultural identity. It is the perfect space within which to address the identity of "consumer." However, a noncritical multiculturalism would serve to obfuscate that identity and the consumer/commodity relationship Edmundson sees in the university, through the presentation of difference that does not openly negotiate that difference. This kind of interrogation is the work of a critical multicultural pedagogy. It is formulated from work done by Paolo Friere in problem-posing education, by Henry Giroux in citizenship education, and by Ira Shor in liberatory education.

American critical multiculturalism focuses on American identity. In this way the focus is placed on the ways in which Americans are different from one another. Practicing these powers of interrogation in the classroom through the use of a critical multicultural pedagogy is far more useful than it is attractive, in that, it is far more than an effective means of engaging, what I will agree with Edmundson in characterizing as, "students who seem rather frightened of their own lives" (1997: 46). Edmundson's essay points up one of the most urgent needs we, as educators, have for a critical multicultural pedagogy. Edmundson argues that as a result of the passing of the baby boomers through the university ("like a fat meal digested by a Boa Constrictor") higher education has become something that parents purchase for their children. As a result the student becomes the consumer of goods and not the imbiber of knowledge her parents were thought to be.

Edmundson's writes, "The Socratic method—the animated, sometimes impolite give and take between student and teacher—seems too jagged for current sensibilities"(45). As a result, Edmundson argues, "Many of the successful professors are the ones who have 'decentered' their classrooms. There's a new emphasis on group projects . . . what [the students] seem to want most is to talk to one another" (45). Edmundson asserts that these learning "environments" allow students to "exchange existing ideas," and he concedes that in the process students may even "change their opinions. But what they generally can't do is acquire a new vocabulary, a new perspective, that will cast issues in a fresh light" (45). This attitude suggests that the young student can attain a new vocabulary by listening to the wisdom of the older professor. Perhaps that exchange needs to move in two directions. It is not the students alone who need to "acquire a new vocabulary." The professor also needs to acquire knowledge from the student. Edmundson bemoans the absence in his classroom of "students from truly poor backgrounds" as if those, or the traditionally marked, "multicultural" others would be the only students whose differences might represent a "truly new vocabulary worth acquiring" (41). All students provide their teachers with the opportunity to learn something new. This has been one of the greatest satisfactions I have received from using a critical multicultural pedagogy.

The move away from what Paolo Friere has termed "banking education" is decentering, it does allow students to talk to each other, it does shift the focus of the classroom from the subject matter to the interpretative processes that can occur in a classroom. A critical multicultural pedagogy is:

Consistent with the liberating purpose of dialogical education, the object of the investigation is not persons (as if they were anatomical fragments), but rather the thought-language with which men and women refer to reality, the levels at which they perceive that reality, and their view of the world, in which their generative themes are found. (Friere, 1993: 78)

The phrase "thought-language" allows for an understanding of the ways in which individuals perceive the world around them. It also allows for the possibility that each individual has some thought-language that is unique to them. It is through this thought-language that individuals compose generative themes. These are the larger ideas around which each one organizes his or her own life, values, and practices, which carry him or her through the world. As Edmundson's essay suggests the new generation of college student is unlike past generations of college students. It is especially crucial that educators make an attempt to understand the thought-language of these students so that we may begin to understand the generative themes around which they are organizing themselves. I am not so sure what we are seeing is simply apathy or depression. It is a shift in cultural consciousness. By clinging to traditional conceptions of education and the traditional relationships between identities, in this case most notably the relationship between student and teacher, we, as educators, are missing opportunities to participate in the formation of the generative themes that will construct the material practices of the twenty-first century.

The opportunity to participate in meaning-making systems of the twenty-first century is impaired by the resistance with which the banking model has been held in place in education systems around the world. Paolo Friere's concept of the "banking education" can be characterized by the following list produced by Friere:

(a) the teacher teaches and the students are taught;
(b) the teacher knows everything and the students know nothing;
(c) the teacher thinks and the students are thought about;
(d) the teacher talks and the students listen—meekly;
(e) the teacher disciplines and the students are disciplined;
(f) the teacher chooses and enforces his choice, and the students comply;
(g) the teacher acts and the students have the illusion of acting through the action of the teacher;
(h) the teacher chooses program content, and the students (who were not consulted) adapt to it;
(i) the teacher confuses the authority of knowledge with his or her own professional authority which she and he sets in opposition to the freedom of the students;
(j) the teacher is the Subject of the learning process, while the pupils are mere objects. (54)

Traditional educational practices, whether they come in the form of "depositing information" into a meek "receptacle" of a student or in the form of eliciting an articulation of resistance from a meek "receptacle" of a student, are noncritical uses of classroom exchange because they cannot function to critique the relationships that serve to reinforce, reproduce, and perpetuate the ideas that are either being deposited or resisted.

Friere argues that the banking concept is used to maintain traditional structures of power. He argues that it is through "banking education" that,

oppressors use their "humanitarianism" to preserve a profitable situation . . . . They care neither to have the world revealed nor to see it transformed. Thus they react instinctively against any experiment which stimulates the critical facilities and is not content with a partial view of reality but always seeks out ties which link one point to another and one problem to another. (54-55)

This helps us to understand how the conflation of American multiculturalism with globalism has become so well entrenched and widely accepted. It also explains the widespread resistance to multiculturalism and the development of a noncritical response to the problems present in American culture. The chain of thought is that there are problems in American culture that need to be interrogated. Those problems are founded in the ways in which difference is perceived and valued in American culture. The differences that are easiest to engage are the visible differences. These differences have traditionally been marked as racial differences. Racial differences are integrally linked with cultural differences. If we look at the cultural differences that produce American culture we threaten the integrity of the fabric of American culture so, instead of focusing on the problems present in American culture due to America's valuation and use of the concept of difference we will look at the differences themselves, all of which can be traced to a space outside of American culture. The focus of the investigation shifts from an examination of the problems present in American culture due to the presence of difference, to the representations of that difference, to the origins of that difference, conveniently located outside of the geographic boundaries of America. In this way the critical gaze is constantly being drawn away from the "profitable situation" that results in American culture through the perpetuation of concepts of difference and the maintenance of the relationships between different subjectivities.

A critical multicultural pedagogy focuses its gaze on the classroom, and within the parameters of that classroom it focuses its gaze upon the relationships that exist within that classroom, and in this process it attempts to teach the student how to gaze critically at him or herself in order to understand the differences that make up his or her own subjectivity. The student can then move to a consideration of how those differences are constructed in relationship to another human being. In this way the student has a model of how to engage difference he or she encounters outside him or herself. This pedagogy, however, requires that the student teach him or herself in many ways. This necessarily means that the relationship between the student and the teacher must change. Decentering the classroom is a multicultural practice that has attempted to achieve student centered learning. It is a useful concept. However, a classroom cannot ever be decentered. The power always rests with the one who gives the grade. This reality must be addressed. Critical multiculturalism is not seeking a world in which students rule and teachers follow. It is a way in which education can "[respond] to the essence of consciousness—*intentionality* . . . . It epitomizes the special characteristic of consciousness: being *conscious of,* not only as intent on objects but as turned in upon itself in a Jasperian "split"—consciousness as consciousness *of* consciousness" (Friere, 1993: 60). Friere's model of liberating education is one that has been translated into the American system of higher education most notably by Ira Shor and Henry Giroux. These liberatory pedagogies, critical multiculturalism included, aim to not only reorganize the ways in which knowledge and education are understood and function in the classroom, but they are also aimed at forming and informing the larger culture. Because students are the material reality of the larger culture, it is reasonable that a liberatory pedagogy, a pedagogy that teaches not only self-awareness but self-reflexivity, is not only useful but necessary for forming future Americans who cannot only make critical judgments but also review, reflect, and readapt those judgments.

What seems fundamental to this kind of development is a shift in understanding of what education is and how it functions. Paolo Friere suggests:

> Education is by nature social, historical, and political.... The idea of an identical and neutral role for all teachers could only be accepted by someone who was either very naive or very clever. Such a person might affirm the neutrality of education, thinking of school as merely a kind of parenthesis whose essential structure was immune to the influences of social class, of gender, or of race. (Shor, 1987: 211)

The concept of a neutral and identical role for teachers performs fixed identity, and limits both the means and the matter of classroom instruction. It is a concept of education as a political action, as an expression of the culture at large, and as a manifestation of the student's participation in sociopolitical practices that a critical multiculturalism implements in the classroom.

In this chapter I offer a model of one critical multicultural classroom. I have implemented the practice of modeling self-reflexivity, self-examination, and self-consciousness as well as the practices of a traditionally decentered classroom in the composition and literature classrooms. In so doing I can emphasize the fluidity of identity that exists within each of my students and within myself. As Friere points out, it is not useful for me to present a pedagogy wherein I mandate the role of all teachers in all classrooms. Each teacher must necessarily take away from this pedagogical model what he or she is comfortable with and what he or she believes will benefit his or her own experience. However, I want to emphasize the role of self-reflexivity. The teacher must interrogate those pieces of the pedagogy he or she takes away and the ways in which he or she uses them. This practice of constant self-reflexivity is the only absolute in the pedagogical model and it does give rise to a constant. It seems that the result of this kind of pedagogy is constant change. My instructional practice changes from class to class. In almost every case students seem to enjoy the freedom to express a variety of aspects of their personalities that this pedagogy affords them. However, they resist changes in me.[1]

Ira Shor has written, "[i]t's a tricky business to organize an untraditional class in a traditional school" (Shor, 1987: 106). The pedagogy I have adapted from work done by Paolo Friere, Henry Giroux, Ira Shor, and Kathleen McCormick interrogates the identity of teacher as well as the identity of student so we can look at the relationships that exist in the classroom. This is not a theory in which students are "thought about"(Friere, 1993: 54). The students in this consideration of critical multicultural pedagogy speak as they do in the classroom. This allows a space in which we can model the myriad relationships that exist outside the classroom where they are expected to become and many times already are thinking, speaking, and acting human beings.

The composition classroom becomes a place wherein the beginning writer can learn to interrogate him or herself as a subject of a variety of discourses because he or she is allowed to understand that "student" is not his or her only identity in the classroom. In other words, when a student steps into the classroom he or she must not subordinate all other facets his or her personality and identity to the one marked "student." When students are allowed to recognize differences within themselves they become open to investigating differences between themselves and others in non-defensive ways. This opens up lines of communication that are difficult to open up in a noncritical multicultural classroom that focuses upon representing difference because it does not force the student into one of two traditional identities. Either the student represents the previously marginalized difference that the noncritical multicultural classroom displays or he or she is the representative of the dominant culture that practices such oppression. Either way, these roles are non-productive.

A critical multicultural pedagogy asks the student to investigate all the identities he or she inhabits in order to allow a variety of perspectives from which he or she can engage a text. This is not an easy pedagogy. The teacher must model these self-reflexive behaviors for the student. This means that the teacher must be willingly to constantly critique his or her relationship with the class, and invite critique of the class by the class. This invitation requires a practical way of allowing students the opportunity to recognize their position of relative power in the class. I can tell students that without learners I cannot be a teacher. However, there must be practices that model this relationship for them. This, in my experience, requires that they become teachers. In and of itself this is a rewarding model that effectively implements the concepts of collaborative work and the decentering of the classroom, however, there is one problem.

This critical multicultural pedagogy may not be effective for what are currently classified as multicultural or non-traditional students. Students in freshman composition classrooms tend to be in the early stages of assimilation, many of them seem to require a great deal of structure and stability in the teacher/student relationship. The disruption caused by an investigation of multiplicity in the classroom is confusing for these students who, by and large, have struggled very hard to simply learn the traditional conventions of classroom practice. They are not ready to critique it.[2] In a way this pedagogy works even on those students who do not remain with the class. They must recognize that the pedagogy is not useful for them and leave the class. This recognition, in and of itself, can be the beginning of a critical awareness of their power to discern their own educational needs.

The "problem" of the "multicultural" student seems to suggest that a noncritical multicultural pedagogy functions to serve an elite student body in order to inform them of the "O"ther at the same time that it assimilates the "O"ther into the culture of the classroom. Critical multiculturalism interrogates the process of assimilation itself. However, this interrogation requires a rather advanced degree of assimilation on the part of the students themselves. In this way a critical multicultural pedagogy resists the noncritical categorization of multicultural students as those students who are marked by racial or cultural difference. Because it calls into question the process of assimilation required to attend college in the first place, it breaks down the process of assimilation to an individual level. Not all students assimilate at the same rate. Not all students can tolerate the shifting identity of the critically multicultural classroom. This recognition reinforces the individuality of those members of the group of human beings we homogenize as students. They all have educational needs and very often they are different from one another in those needs. This foregrounds difference that is not racially or ethnically marked and reinforces a concept of culture that is based on practices that constantly shift to meet the needs of the culture. In this way the mere presence of a critical multicultural classroom in the curriculum impacts the awareness of students both in and out of the classroom.

In the classroom, the critical multicultural pedagogy must address both the needs presented by the culture of the classroom and the needs of the culture of the university. In his essay "Monday Morning Fever," Shor suggests constructing a class whose major components are generative themes and collaborative work (adapted from Friere's literacy model) (Shor, 1987: 106). Building on Shor's work, I found that collaborative work was essential in helping the students find a space in which they could hear their own voices and then learn to hear the voices of others without the fear of "being wrong" that often causes an individual to take a defensive stance. Moreover, this method of work must also allow students to move away from their concentration on me—the teacher—as the "one who knows" in the classroom. By decentering the authority in the classroom, *and* privileging multiple voices we can hear a dialogue in the classroom. When the voices in the classroom become parts of a dialogue, the privileged position of knowledge constantly shifts from one voice to another. One voice is the authority only until it is challenged by another voice. It is important that the teacher's voice is just one among the many (although this really is not easy to achieve, if it is at all possible, but the attempt is important and poignant). This dynamic begins a series of shifts away from traditional models of classroom practice.

Generative themes are ideas that students recognize as part of their own experience and thus allow the student to feel an immediate mastery of the topic (1987: 106). The use of generative themes allows the class to move beyond a more traditional concern with the mastery of literary topics or grammar to a consideration of how literary topics and grammar function in the context of the student's life. This achieves dual objectives. The students learn the traditions of literary study and the conventions of academic writing and at the same time they learn how that knowledge affects them on an individual level.

Placing a value on the ways in which the students incorporate this knowledge into their lives is no more difficult or subjective than grading is in a traditional classroom. "Are we being graded as cultural artifacts or what?" asked Deborah. I explained that I would grade according to the standard criteria: coherence, clarity, grammar, idea development, participation and attendance. What was being changed was the way we understood "standard criteria," so that the syllabus and my grading practices, as well as their reading, writing, thinking, and speaking skills were all up for review. I asked the students to keep a running critique on my instruction and the syllabus. For her final exam essay Susan, wrote,

Our English 1C class was very non-traditional in many ways. Students taught the class on many occasions, we were not just lectured to and expected to regurgitate facts on a test, and we were often forced to find answers to difficult questions by ourselves. However, in some ways [we had to hold on to] certain traditions.

Grading happens to be one of the traditions we could not get away from. This is a common thread in all of the responses. They felt I was "fair" and, as one student wrote, "as long as there is a place called a classroom and a person called a teacher there should be things called grades." I attempted to be as democratic in the grading process as possible. I used presentation critiques to grade the presentations, and I allowed for one essay on the final exam to be a discussion of the problematic of each particular collaborative group. I did this so the students could let me know if they felt one person did more work and thus deserved a larger share of the collaborative grade than another group member deserved deserved. I was surprised at the equanimity in those essays. While in the beginning, no one in the class liked doing collaborative work, one student wrote, "For once the responsibility of the entire project was not on me. I never felt overwhelmed because I knew I wasn't alone." The primary reason given for the unanimous dislike of the collaborative work effort was actually a deep distrust of other students' study habits. This was an interesting problem that we struggled with all quarter, and one which was never really resolved. The students set aside their distrust to do the class work. However, many of them left the class with the same feeling they had come in with; some people simply work harder than others do.

The bulk of student grades in a critically multicultural course come from collaborative work done in the form of a class presentation, critiques of those "presentations", and a final research project, which develops out of class discussion and revolves around a generative theme. The class presentation is not just a fifteen-minute recital; the presenting group is responsible for leading class. On that day the student becomes the teacher. I do not introduce them; I do not frame their presence in any formal sense. I ask the students to write a draft of their teaching plan to see if they are missing anything that might embarrass them, and to make sure they have enough material to run a thirty-minute class with twenty minutes of discussion. In this draft they have to "begin when they walk in the door." That is they need to script their performance as though it were their classroom because on that day it is. I also encourage the students to be as creative as possible. That is effective from both a critically multicultural perspective and the perspective of a writing teacher. The objective is to engage the audience and make clear to them the idea the group is presenting in the clearest terms possible. Each group is critiqued in writing by every other student, and the teaching group is responsible for writing a self-critique of themselves. This way we have ongoing feedback regarding what has been done in class. Because I consider the feedback given in the critiques when I assign the grade for the class "presentation", I believe this model also allows the student to understand his or her own involvement in the production of knowledge. The shift from the teacher as the primary "giver of grades" and the student as the one who receives a grade is a resultant shift away from a more traditional classroom paradigm.[3] However, it is not an unproblematic shift.

In the model class that I will be using to make specific references to the concepts I am discussing in this chapter, the students were told that I was implementing an experimental pedagogy and that their responses would be part of my documentation of the result of my attempt to implement it. For this class the generative was multiculturalism.[4] At the beginning of the class I asked all of the students to write a one-page, 250-word essay on multiculturalism.[5] Many of them felt that they understood the concept, but what they wrote described some mysterious form of benevolence that came from somewhere in order to make the world fair. I asked the students to write this same essay as part of the final exam. Following ten weeks of consideration, many of them realized that they had not previously considered multiculturalism as a theory that really touched their own lives. Many final exam essays revealed that the students' understanding of the topic had changed dramatically from their first essays. As part of his final exam, Mark, an Anglo-American student wrote:

At the beginning of the quarter when I was asked to define the term multiculturalism, I wrote a one page paper that I thought adequately addressed the question. The definition that I gave was that multiculturalism was the idea of many cultures living together . . . . Now I would say that multi-culturalism . . . [is] a learning concept that forces the student to explore the situation around [him]. It makes a person analyze the effect that their culture and the institutions that they are a part of have on them. Basically, the understanding I have of multiculturalism is that it doesn't allow students to go through their education close minded [*sic*].

Mark's response illustrates the depth of thought many of the students in this class reached. I feel that it is a result of their ability to interact with the topic on their own terms using their own "thought-language" to work through the concept presented to them. Mark's willingness to consider a shift in his own thinking is representative of the personal investment these students had in their work.

There was a great deal of writing in this classroom. The students were broken up into groups of three based upon a shared interest as articulated in a one-page, 250 word justification for the topic of their choice. Each group had to write a five-page rough draft of their class presentation. Each student wrote a one-page, 250 word critique of each presentation, and the presenting group wrote a self-critique of the same length. The final collaborative effort was a seven-to ten-page research paper with a minimum of five outside sources that did not include the primary text. While difficult for the students, these papers illustrate some of the strongest writing skills I have ever seen in an undergraduate-level paper. The arguments were complex and sophisticated because they were the result of a ten-week-long conversation. In essence every project had the feedback of every student in the class. Therefore, every project went through multiple stages of thinking and writing. It is in this way that the critical multicultural classroom uses Friere's problem-posing pedagogy. The students learn that the world is not "static reality, but . . . a reality in process, a transformation . . . . Problem-posing education affirms men and women as beings in the process of *becoming"*(Friere, 1993: 65). This is an especially salient approach in the freshman composition class. However, it also allows the student to realize that there are myriad answers to any given task. It opens up possibility and allows students to understand that they choose to believe and support certain beliefs in the face of others. It also allows them to understand that knowledge happens everywhere and not only in the context of a classroom and in relationship with a teacher. This widens the scope of possibility inherent in decisions they make in their participation in the wider culture.

In terms of citizenship education widening the perspective of the world allows the student of the critical multicultural classroom to "[generate] new categories and [raise] new questions that could not be raised in [the traditional classroom]"(Giroux, 1983: 170). This is because the student is asked to consider the ways they participate in cultural institutions instead of simply accepting their position(s) within them as passive observers. This is foreground in the collaborative groupwork. I stress the word collaborative.

The groupwork was not traditional—non-traditional—collaboration. The students were not grouped together in order to respond to a teacher's prompt and be contained by teacher guidelines. Students wrote collaborative guidelines specific to their own group at the beginning of the project. Subsequent experience has shown me just how crucial this practice is. It seems to alleviate some of the anxiety members of the class feel regarding the skills of their group members. More than simply an anxiety relieving practice, it is crucial that the groups make a social contract with one another. In these classrooms we are investigating difference; we have not yet solved that problem, therefore, clearly articulated guidelines for behavior between group members, each possessing his or her own idea of how the group should work, is crucial.

Each group, makes rules that apply to how many absences the

group will allow before they could request that the absent person be dropped from the group, and they also assign tasks to ensure equal labor distribution. Traditional classrooms tend to value the work of the individual and thereby set the students in competition with one another. This precludes open sharing of information and work as they are all trying to get and keep an edge on one another. The critical multicultural classroom asks that the end product be the result of shared labors. We are all invested in the project and therefore we are all responsible for the outcome. Negotiating the differences in perceptions, abilities, and study habits is one way that we can begin to shift our analytical focus from the specter of our difference to a closer scrutiny of the relationships that exist as a result of those differences.

For me, the goal of that first class was to test out a conception of non-hierarchized knowledge, non-privileged texts, and the multiplicitous ways in which both knowledge and text function in a classroom. In order to meet this agenda, I felt that the students had to understand that they had some degree of power in the classroom. When we began with an essay entitled, "The Classroom and the Wider Culture: Identity as a Key to Learning English Composition," written by Fan Shen, the conversation really took a turn I did not expect.[6] I started by talking about the way the study questions at the end of the essay reinforced traditional ways of reading about difference in that they do not foreground how difference is constituted and reproduced.[7] The students took control of the conversation with a dialogue concerning the ways their personal identities were constructed and the ways this construction was different from the constructions of their social/cultural identity. We spoke only tangentially about the text, but the students were able to refer back to it when I asked them to show me how their ideas worked in the text. In a more traditional classroom the value of the reading may be more focused on the student's understanding of the writer's argument; in other words, an accurate gauge of the student's understanding of a text is traditionally proven by way of summary. By traditional standards of summarizing the writer's point, we did not get very far. However, I felt this was a very fruitful discussion. We had already begun to move toward a critical multicultural understanding of the text by focusing on the moments of difference in the text and by having a dialogue that discussed the ways the illustrations of difference represented by the text could be seen by the students as a part of their own lived experience.

It is important that all of the students in the class began to interrogate the ways in which they had been constructed in order to represent a specific cultural group. "White" students began to interrogate what it meant to be constructed as "white," and this allowed us to begin understanding a dominant "white" culture as one cultural category among many others very early in the process. This shift in understanding a "dominant" culture in its often uninterrogated position of privilege subjects it to the same kinds of questions any other set of cultural values and positions might encounter. What is more important is that a shift in relationships occurred during this class discussion. The students were speaking and I was listening and learning from and about them. Their relationships with the cultural group upon which they depended, in part, for their identity had begun to shift. Cultural identity became a topic or issue to be discussed among other topics and issues. They were informing me of their experiences with this phenomenon and I was (really) learning from the information they provided. This shift in the traditional student/teacher relationship, coupled with other exercises of liberty within the room, allowed the students to experience a sense of power in the room. However, with this power came resistance.

Michel Foucault has been recorded in an interview entitled, "Space, Knowledge and Power," as having said,

> [N]othing irritates me as much as these inquiries . . . on the foundations of power in a society or the self-institution of a society . . . . These are not fundamental phenomena. There are only reciprocal relations, and the perpetual gaps between intentions in relation to one another. (Foucault, 1984b: 247)

Later in this essay he talks about describing figures "through whom power passed or are important in the fields of power relations" (247). Finally in talking about oppression and liberty Foucault says that: "Liberty is a practice" (245). Liberatory education and empowering students have been the topics of a large amount of multicultural work in the past ten years. Power cannot be possessed or passed about. It exists in relationships and passes through individuals in particular relationships and in given historical moments. However, it can be exercised, and it can shift. During these moments, when the students were explaining the relationships between themselves and the text, and the relationship between the text and the ideas they had found in it, a relationship existed between student and teacher within which power had shifted and the possibility that anyone and everyone in the room could exercise that power occurred. This is the result of implementing practices that engage students in discussions of classroom governance, designing group guidelines, and of choosing topics for discussion. These pedagogical strategies allow them to practice liberty. The experience of liberty allows them to move into a position that allows them to access the power in the classroom.

When I felt that they were feeling powerful enough not to cave under my dictates, I handed out the multicultural reading paradigm that I had adapted from Kathleen McCormick's book, *The Culture of Reading and The Teaching of English*, and I asked the students to reread the Fan Shen essay in terms of that paradigm. It was at this time that I realized that the students were resisting utilizing the power available to them in the classroom. The resistance began in earnest around the topic of reading. The class began to discuss how the multicultural paradigm differed from a more traditional concept of reading.

McCormick's work begins with a review of the ways in which reading has culturally been regarded as an unproblematic practice until quite recently, and

yet despite the increasing emphasis on the reader's background, on varying contexts of reading, and on reading as a process. The "commonsensical", objectivist model, which assumes that reading is a skill and that texts "contain" information that skilled readers should simply take in and "comprehend" correctly, still dominates much teaching and research. (McCormick, 1994: 3)

A critical multiculturalism teaches students to question traditional knowledge. The idea of a reader as a passive participant is an expedient used by traditional instruction in its most simplistic practice. In the critical multicultural classroom we must hold out for the probability that there are multiple readings of any given text. Further we must understand that these multiplicitous readings are not the result but the beginning of a conversation that can lead to meaningful conclusions. Reading a text demands individual interpretations of a work in order to allow each reader to interpret the differences between the interpretations.

The Fan Shen essay opened up the class to the possibility that the student was not simply a receptor in the practice of reading but an active participant. When class reconvened, we looked at the way in which even a progressive text such as *Signs of Life* played into the traditional concept of reading. We examined the questions at the end of the reading and deconstructed the way they worked. We then discussed the "multicultural" reading paradigm that I had adapted from McCormick (see appendix). However, at this point I was doing all the talking. My journal of that time period shows that the students were passive at best and reticent for the most part. I continued to engage them by turning the discussion away from the topic of their traditional reading practices to focus on the critical multicultural reading practices. I explained that I had designed the multicultural reading paradigm because I wanted to help them understand how an examination of the text through the reader puts the reader into a reciprocal relationship with the text. Instead of expecting that knowledge has been transmitted from the text to the student, the multicultural reading paradigm asks what the student has read—not what the text said. This seems like a matter of semantics, but it is actually a shifting paradigm that tells the reader that he or she has some agency in the reception of a text. The text does not simply mean, it means in relationship to the reader in a particular context, at a particular historical moment.[8] I was not prepared for the overwhelming resistance I met when the class reconvened.

The students had listened to me. However, they let me know at the next class that they were uncomfortable with the concept of privileging themselves as readers. They wanted the text to mean inherently. They wanted an author who knows and transmits knowledge, and they really wanted a teacher to tell them what it means. It was unsettling for them to entertain the concept that there is no one who "knows." The construction of knowledge as an ongoing discussion within a given discourse community seemed to make most of the students uncomfortable. I believe that this discomfort stems from the effect that this shift (in their understanding of the way knowledge is constructed) had upon their understandings of their position in the academy. Their expectation up to this point was to imbibe knowledge and return it in a recognizable form to the teacher. The possibility that they were themselves producers of knowledge and participants in the production of certain kinds of knowledge was alarming to some. I explained, as McCormick writes, that a student in a critical multicultural classroom must learn to recognize "herself as a social subject neither fully determined by the culture of which [he or she is a] part nor simply individuals who can become "free" of the dominant cultural ideology"(McCormick, 1994:7). This idea of being both producer of and produced by ideology brings us to a consideration of the relationship between power and responsibility. This was a relationship with which we struggled for the next three weeks. This paradigm shift allowed the students to begin to struggle with concepts that they thought they simply had to accept about the way in which the world functions, such as, racism, sexism, and elitism, which in college freshman terms translate into, segregated student clubs, date rape, and the Greek system. However, the class was still unclear about how that power was supposed to work in the classroom.

Once we began to deconstruct the reading process, we also began to deconstruct the classroom. The first day of group meetings, the first Friday of the quarter, did look like Bedlam, and the students were very concerned that they, and I think I, did not know what was going on. A student named Sandra wrote in her one of her final exam essays:

After being introduced to the idea of this multi-cultural format, I decided to stick with the class and give it a try. I felt that the idea sounded like a nice change. I still do, except that there were a few times when I felt really frustrated and confused. I felt that often Lesliee seemed quite unorganized. However, I did not see this as a reflection of her teaching ability at all, but due to the fact that this was something new to all of us. Success will come from trial and error, and our class was doing just that.

Very often I found myself struggling with the feeling that I had lost control. Once I realized that this was a response to the actual lack of control that existed—that I had designed into the class—I began to relax. The first day of group meetings was not actually as disorganized as it had appeared to be. I met with group one and they were well prepared for their class presentation of David Hwang's *M. Butterfly*. Group two was on its way, but they did not believe it. Group three was reconfigured because we lost a student, and so was Group five. At this point in the quarter I had twelve out of eighteen students who attended faithfully and participated fully. They seemed excited about the work even if a little dubious as to how it would turn out.

The first day of group presentations resistance was performed. I walked into a class of about nine students who were looking at me with stricken faces. I asked them what was "up," and they just looked at each other—then I noticed. Only one member of the presenting group was present. So I said to Simon, "Well, do you want to lead the class? I will help you." He agreed and began a very well thought through response to the element of homosexuality in *M. Butterfly*.[9] He was scared, but he persevered. About twenty minutes into the presentation the other two group members—consistently active students—came in. They offered no excuses, and I made no move to acknowledge that anything out of place had occurred. They took their places at the front of the class and continued with the presentation.[10]

When the presentation was finished the presenting group had some trouble eliciting responses from the class. At this point—as John said—I put in my eight cents. I made the problem the focal point of the discussion (Shor), I asked them to think about how both Gallimard and Song in *M. Butterfly* were trapped by social constructions which they, for one reason or another, could not escape, I suggested that we all knew what that felt like because of what had happened in class. I asked, "Why were you all so stricken when Luna and Ruby were not present?" They would not respond, so I answered for them, saying that it was probably because the structure of the class had fallen apart. I suggested that they had all looked to me to rebuild it. However, the room belonged to Simon. I could help as could they, but it was his room. When he began his "lecture" he looked to the class for feedback, he even asked who had done the reading and no one responded. I then chastised them: "Those of you who did not do the reading were sheepish and did not want to admit it because you knew your participation at this point was crucial." In hindsight, I believe that I was as stricken as they were.

The students resisted exercising power in the classroom because they did not believe they could. I resisted and then finally did exercise power in the classroom because I felt I had to. This is a crucial moment in Friere's problem-posing pedagogy. He writes that, "[D]ialogue cannot occur between those who deny others the right to speak . . . and those whose right to speak have been denied them . . . . Those who have been denied their primordial right to speak their word must first reclaim this right and prevent the continuation of this dehumanizing aggression"(Friere, 1993: 69). Friere is suggesting that the relationship between student and teacher in the traditional model of education or the "banking" method is one of she who cannot speak and she who can speak for others. This is not to say that the student is literally silenced but her words are "empty....[and] cannot denounce the world"(69). Without this ability to speak one cannot act and without the ability to act one cannot transform the world. This was vividly illustrated by my exhortation to act in which I not only spoke to the class but also answered for them.

I used the power I had in the class to try to assure them that they could also have power in the class. However, I think I brow beat them a little when I did it. I realized what had happened and I reverted to the Socratic method. I asked the class to think about the ways in which they participate or fail to participate in producing the structure of the class. I asked them to consider the ways in which the actions of the individual affect the group and the ways in which the community or group affects the behavior of the individual.[11] I asked them to think about how they function in these ways in both the classroom and the larger social structure they inhabit. And, finally, I wanted them to consider what any of this had to do with writing and thinking critically and multiculturally.

I was quite disheartened by what I perceived to be my abandonment of the project by grabbing the reins of power one second after they had flown free. Therefore, I was very pleased when I noticed a flyer on my way to class the next week. There was a conference regarding welfare reform and California's Proposition 187.[12] In conjunction with the conference there was a panel led by students that debated strategies of student-led protest. Thinking that knowledge comes from different places and because the issues seemed relevant to our class topic, I went into the classroom and suggested that we all attend the panels. The students were astounded at first, but we took a vote and left the classroom. This practice of liberty seems to have built upon the previous failure to exercise power in the class and the students responded to this venture quite vigorously.

Susan, Mark, and John attended a talk on welfare reform with me, and the rest of the class went to the student-organizing panel. The overall effect of taking the class to the lectures was that they began to feel more comfortable privileging their position as interpreter/reader. The next class began with a short bout of critiquing the speakers, but then the class began to discuss the ways in which going to the panel allowed them to understand that the work we were doing in class was directly applicable to the outside world. We used the multicultural reading paradigm to deconstruct the panel arguments and to discuss not only the arguments but also the student responses to the arguments. I asked the students to write a critique of the panel they had attended. In response to the panel on student organized protest, John, an African American student, wrote that he had begun to understand that "it becomes a personal task to find . . . information that allows me to find my identity." John was one of the first students to exercise power in the class, and he was a wonderful model for the rest of the class. John's comment illustrates his conscious awareness of his power to define himself in relationship to the identity he carried most significantly as an African American male.

The class discussion on the panel issues was heartening, had I been following a more traditional syllabus, I do not believe I would have allowed myself that serendipitous moment and I would have lost a valuable teaching tool. However, the next two sessions were tedious and the students seemed even more resistant. They were all present and participating, and we never again suffered the absenteeism of the presenters. It was three class meetings later that I was late to class. I opened the door and found that class had started without me! Group four explained to me afterward that when the bell rang and I was not there they figured it was their class and it really should not matter if I was present or not. They were glad to see me, but they understood that they had the power to share their knowledge with the class independent of a "teacher" being present. They were the teachers. This turn of events really seems to have shifted the class dynamic, and we were ready, then, to return to a consideration of our generative theme: what had any of this to do with critical multiculturalism and writing?

A large part of the class involved reading Maxine Hong

Kingston's *China Men*. I chose the book because it was a "multicultural" text in the current understanding of that term. It is written by a Chinese American woman, and among many other topics it deals with the narrator's construction of a family history. In the course of her search, however, the narrative brings up many questions about American history, history versus personal narrative, the terms of subjectivity, which make sense within American ideology, and the concept of coherent identity itself. For their group presentation, Robert and Kaleb (their group had lost a member) asked that everyone form a circle with their chairs, and then they presented the ways in which they saw the themes of capitalism and communism working in Kingston's description of the male relatives in the chapter, "On the Making of More Americans."

The suggestion that the class move around in the classroom was a first. No other group had done so prior to this presentation. It is a compelling example of Foucault's argument about the relationship between space and power. Robert and Kaleb appropriated the space of the teacher not by standing at the front of the room as a traditional teacher would, and as all the other groups had. They exercised power by utilizing a strategy that traditional teaching understands as a mechanism that attempts to shift power in the space of the classroom. Foucault writes of the changing form of the modern state that it became apparent that, "if one govern[s] too much, one [does] not govern at all"(Foucault, 1984b: 242). By placing the students in a circle Robert and Kaleb mimicked the strategy of liberal education and in so doing exercised complete power over the class, myself included.

The class was impressed by the circle idea, and Robert, an Anglo American student, and Kaleb, an Afghanistani student, received high marks in the class critiques for an intelligent and innovative presentation. Their presentation really opened up the class. Robert and Kaleb not only opened up a space for a pointed discussion of the relationship between critical multiculturalism, and writing but they also helped me to understand the teacher function in a class based on the concept of critical multiculturalism. The conversation turned to the ways in which the differences between capitalism and communism had always been represented in the students' life experiences. We then took another look at different moments in the text when participation in either capitalist economy or communist economy was represented. The students were quite frustrated to find that we could not decipher an authorial indication of one being a monolith of "bad" or "good" but that both seemed to be problematic. The relationship between Kingston's writing technique and the ways in which Robert and Kaleb interpreted her work foreground capitalism as one of many economy systems. This allowed for a discussion of the "American" economic system that many "white" Americans do not actively see as one among many, but as the primary means of social organization.

We then moved to a discussion of how difference within the United States is constructed. This was a deep ideological discussion coming from a freshman composition class. We all agreed that "difference is in the eye of the definer" and that the definition always had to be questioned. I suppose there are easier ways to get a class to reach this understanding, but I believe that the students reached this agreement on their own. It was their knowledge they made together in that room, and it was therefore that much more valuable to them. We began to wonder out loud how Kingston's work caused us to have such a theoretical and ideological discussion regarding what looked like three simple tales about three Chinese uncles.

I explained to the class that I felt the value of Maxine Hong Kingston's work was that she seems to be aware of the ways in which language is used to construct difference, and therefore she can represent difference in her own text not as a monolithic reality but as a constantly shifting dialogue (see chapter three). When we read for difference as well as about difference we can appreciate the ways in which those differences are represented. When a writer writes a story that allows a reader to understand a text in a number of different ways, we, as a culture, very often name that author a "good" author. Kingston's work allows us to read in her text not only differences that may be understood in terms of American culture; we can also read the ways differences might be represented in terms of a culture that may not be our own. We found or produced in our readings and negotiations of our readings of the text a model for our own critical multicultural classroom. We learned that thinking about ourselves in relationship with others in the room allowed us to focus on the ways in which differences shaped those relationships. When we focused on the relationship we could see that the differences were sometimes constructions of difference that we did not support or understand as difference, but had assimilated from the larger culture. We saw how we constructed differences ourselves in order to separate us from them.

Robert and Kaleb's presentation also brought to light the teacher function in the critical multicultural classroom. There was no escaping the authority that I had in the room, but the students' comments indicate that they had experienced power in the class. Simon wrote in his final essay, "Lesliee did a good job . . . she gave away as much of the power as she could although she had a hard time letting students run their own presentation. She always had to cut in to keep them going down the right path." This is quite an astute statement. This indicates that Simon was feeling an infringement upon his own power in the classroom. Many times I felt exactly like I was cutting in to make the conversation go where it "needed" to go in spite of the fact that I was saying that the students were responsible for taking us where we "needed" to go. I wanted to teach them that they are responsible for initiating and responding to dialogic possibilities. If someone poses a question they are obligated to posit a response. I tried to take away notions of right and wrong answers in order to limit the possibility of censorship, but all of this required a lot of teaching, which meant I spent a lot of time talking. This means I exercised most of the power in the room in spite of my self-reflexive attempts to allow the students to practice liberty and exercise their own power.

In the case of Kaleb and Robert's presentation, however, I had allowed Kaleb to use one of the papers he had written for another class to foreground the discussion of capitalism and communism. He showed me the "A" paper he had written in his political science class and I allowed him to refer to his own research as a means of supporting his reading of Kingston's text. This, coupled with the interesting use of the space of the classroom, allowed me the opportunity to "sit back" and become a student in the group. I was also lulled by the liberal approach of the circle. I experienced it as a practice of liberty, and I felt free from being the voice of authority in the room. It was phenomenal, the quality of the conversation was invigorating and the insights we reached as a class surpassed anything I could have hoped for. It was then that I realized that my function in a critical multicultural classroom is truly a non-traditional one; it is to allow myself to become a student again. It is to allow myself the freedom to negotiate the border between two traditionally oppositional identities. As Michelle said following her own presentation, "you know, you have to be a really good student to be a really good teacher."

A critical multicultural pedagogy helps students to understand "men and women as beings in the process of becoming—as unfinished, uncompleted beings in and with a likewise unfinished reality" (Friere, 1993: 65). Friere's problem-posing pedagogy foregrounds the constant shifting of identity in a constantly shifting reality. This recognition opens a space within which a static and constant identity can be read as a practice that shuts down possibility and limits power and liberty. A critical multicultural pedagogy asks not only the student but also the teacher as well to learn how to interrogate him or herself and his or her relationship to the culture at large. This interrogation allows for the production of a self-aware critical knowledge and allows for the development of the skills that are required to interact at that complex level of thought. At a material level, teaching critical literacy results in sharper interpretive skills and sophisticated writing skills in the students. Paolo Friere noted in his "Letter to North American Teachers" that, "reading and writing words encompasses the reading of the world" (Shor, 1987: 212). The multicultural, multidimensional reality of the United States demands new reading and writing skills: a multicultural pedagogy that does not simply present difference as difference but reads for the ways in which difference is produced and represented. A critical multicultural pedagogy can begin to reproduce the dominant culture as one category of cultural reality among many cultural categories. This shift allows a student to investigate the relationships between those categories, and in this way we can begin to produce students who are capable of writing a new dialogue with which they can begin to address and redress these representational practices. In this way I hope to participate in the production of what Henry Giroux refers to as "both a 'school of thought' and a process of critique" (Giroux, 1983: 8). That is, through the use of critical theory I hope to produce critically literate students. These students will respond to these practices in ways that will allow practitioners and theorists alike to see what needs to be addressed next in the attempt to produce "new historical conditions" that can meet the needs of a multiplicitous American culture (41).

As the endnotes to this chapter indicate, a constant concern of mine was the problem of addressing the needs of the traditionally marked "multicultural" student. The critical multicultural classroom it seems is not as non-traditional as one would have hoped in that it still seems to function as a mechanism of accommodation and it still serves a homogeneous body of "traditional" students. The problems connected with the incorporation of "non-traditional" or "multicultural" students into a classroom that utilizes this pedagogy are not insoluble. However, a shift in focus seems requisite. The ways in which those students marked "different" have been marked, as "different," must be examined. The ways in which they have been trained to think of themselves as "good" or "bad" students, as "traditional" or "non-traditional," and as "multicultural" or "American" must be examined.

The students in that first class were multicultural in that they are representative of the many different cultural groups that make up American culture. However, they were monocultural in that they had all been trained to understand their traditional roles as students. They understood academic convention even if they had not yet mastered it, and, more importantly, they wanted to master academic convention. This leads me to believe that the definition of "multiculturalism" as reliant upon a representation factor is not useful to either the student or the teacher. A critical multicultural education must be multifaceted. I have offered only one model. Simple representation, even when it investigates and encourages multiplicitous responses, cannot be the only means of engaging a student.

NOTES

1. This is not an opportunity for psychotic shifts of personality. Each time I change my approach in the classroom it is a result of considering the efficacy of such change and it is not a unilateral change. The students are always part of the change. I discuss with them my concerns and my proposal for change and they participate in the decision-making process with me. They sometimes find this very disconcerting. They are used to a teacher who makes unilateral decisions. This alleviates them from all responsibility for their education. If they "don't learn anything" it is difficult to place all the blame on the teacher. Some may argue that students are incapable of "knowing what they need." This is an expedient for eschewing any power a student may bring to a classroom. In this chapter I illustrate that students, by and large, possess a clear knowledge of what they need.

2. I lost two students who were second-language speakers. This alarmed me because theoretically, I was developing this pedagogy to accommodate them. They both told me they were uncomfortable with the lack of traditional structure in the classroom and that the level of the conversation bewildered them.

3. At the end of this chapter there is an appendix that contains documents referred to in the text. Those documents are class syllabus, multicultural reading paradigm, collaborative work guidelines, a comparison between traditional reading strategies and a critical multicultural reading paradigm, and a copy of the final exam.

4. I want to thank the students in this class for allowing me to use their classroom for this attempt to construct a critical multicultural pedagogy, and for allowing me to use their voices as critical evidence in this text. This classroom was registered as experimental with the University of California, Riverside.

5. I had actually chosen this theme prior to the class because I wanted to try to teach a multicultural class that fit my redefinition of that term. That is, an understanding of difference that does not rely on traditional physiological markers of difference. This is not what Shor means when he talks about generative themes. He actually goes into the class without a syllabus and has the class develop the generative theme. Out of that conversation he designs a syllabus. Since this first class I have followed Shor's model of asking the students to help construct the syllabus for the course. This practice meets with

more or less success depending upon the group of students in the class.

6. This essay is concerned with the incongruence between the conventions of academic writing instruction expected of a student in the Chinese educational system and the expectations of the American educational system. Fan Shen ties these expectations into the concept of cultural identity and the ways in which a writer can only express him or herself through the definitions of his or her identity that have been developed through a relationship to a larger culture. These definitions, Shen argues, are reinforced through the conventions of academic writing instruction. When the writer's cultural identity shifts by dint of a geographic relocation, this shift in identity comes into direct conflict with the new writing convention. One example that the essay offers is that in Chinese academic writing the convention is to deflect the onus of the writing from the individual. In this way, the Chinese writer new to American convention could be very uncomfortable using the personal pronoun I. This essay can be found in *Signs of Life*.

7. These questions are listed in the appendix. I produced a handout that compares and contrasts the questions contained in *Signs of Life* (page 494) with the questions I developed in my "critical multicultural reading paradigm" (also included in the appendix).

8. Since teaching this first class I have encountered some criticism regarding the reading paradigm. It has been suggested that it is merely reader response in another guise. It is true that this reading paradigm is very similar to reader response. However, while reader response reads for a meaning, a critical multicultural reading paradigm reads for a multiplicity of interpretations. Each class will come to its own conclusion as to meaning based upon a discussion of the interpretations presented by the individual members of the class. This allows students the liberty to express their own idiosyncratic views of a text and the power to exchange those views with others. To some of my critics this looks like Bedlam. Sometimes it feels that way. However, it allows me to compensate for my seemingly inescapable urge to "prepare" a class plan that homogenizes all my classes. Each class is different because I attempt to allow for all the differences present in them. Sometimes this does call for thinking on my feet.

9. This text produced a great deal of discussion regarding the ways in which gender is constructed. The students could not believe Gallimard did not know that Song was a male. We discussed the ways in which his recognition was irrelevant because what mattered was how he constructed himself in relationship to Song. He was a man to her woman, he was a Frenchman to her exotic Chinese, and he was powerful in the presence of her frailty. We then looked at Song as a figure of strength and this allowed us to consider the weakness of Gallimard. In this way we could see the ways in which the characters constructed themselves as different from and for one another. We could also read for the ways in which Hwang constructed difference in his narrative as an ever-shifting relationship between constructions of self.

10. I did not acknowledge their late entry because I felt that to do so

would disrupt Simon's presentation. I also wanted to hold discussion of their lateness for a general class discussion that could be held separate from the presentation. It has been suggested to me that I should have reprimanded these young women. However, this runs counter to the philosophy of the classroom. Their obligation was to the class. They have no obligation to me to attend. I felt that a general class discussion was important in this first test of the stability of the experimental classroom, and that I had to allow the class to voice their responses to what appeared to me to be a flagrant disregard of the obligations these young women had made to their group and to the class.

11. This was really the only comment I made about student attendance and participation aside from the comments I made while assigning them the task of designing group guidelines. I feel that responsibility can be legislated but not enforced. I cannot coerce students to attend class. If they are to understand their own volition, in terms of learning, they must take the responsibility for attending the class upon themselves. This concept of being responsible for one's own education and respecting one's obligation to other members of the class was the idea I tried to convey during this particular class discussion.

12. This is a fairly infamous proposition that passed but is currently being appealed. This proposition will seriously limit the public services available to unauthorized immigrants. Because of California's high population of legal Mexican immigrants, and Chicano/as, this proposition has been interpreted as an attempt to specifically control illegal Mexican immigration. Although, its wording addresses any and all human beings that have immigrated to the United States illegally and attempt to participate in public services offered in California.

Appendix: Multicultural Reading Paradigm

(This format has been adapted from a format presented by Kathleen McCormick in *The Culture of Reading and the Teaching of English, page 157*.)

1. *What is your first response(s) to the text?*
Consider emotional responses to subject matter, and technical or emotional responses to the organization or presentation of the subject matter. Are you bored, angry, confused, or intrigued?

2. *What do you think caused your response(s)?* You must consider many things in order to answer this question:
Subject matter: Have you been culturally trained to find certain ideas presented in the text to be offensive? Are the "social norms" (cultural training) of the characters similar or different to your own, are they similar or different to those values represented by the narrator? Are you familiar with the historical setting of the story or the history to which the story refers?
Textual structure: Is this story being told in a story format that is familiar to you? How are you used to being told a story? Do you find that the story format works well with the story or are you distracted by the incongruence? What kinds of characters are present in the story? Are these the types of characters you are used to reading about? Do you have knowledge of the literary history that either the format of the story or the characterizations of the performers represents?
Personal taste: Perhaps you prefer murder mysteries, have you responded in this way because it is simply not your favorite kind of reading? What is your favorite kind of reading? How has this preference

been instilled in you—who or what circumstances taught you to read your favorite types of work? Did the story "play out" the way you expected it to—were you "tricked" by the ending? Why might this have happened?

Reading instruction: If the ending surprised you was it because of the cultural values portrayed or was it because the author used a writing convention that you are unfamiliar with? What literary conventions were used that you were familiar with? Do you enjoy those conventions, agree with them or disagree with? For instance—is the "bad girl" always depicted in terms of darkness? You may find that you are familiar with more literary conventions than you had previously thought and that you simply disregard them because you disagree with them—engage with this internal negotiation and describe it for your reader.

3. *Can you formulate a critical response to the text?*
This question asks you to formulate a unified narrative response to the text you have read. It wishes for you to speak as objectively as possible about the text in terms of its relationship to you as a reader, and to the cultural, historical moment that produced it. This is a difficult maneuver for the beginning critic and we will work on it together in class. In order to move toward a critical formulation, bring questions to class that sound like this: Why would character X act in such a way? When was this thing written? Who is the author? Why don't I like character Z? Why did it have to end that way?

GUIDELINES FOR COLLABORATIVE WRITING

(Adapted from guidelines presented by Kathleen McCormick *The Culture of Reading and the Teaching of English*.)

- Each group must discuss and agree upon an attendance policy. How many absences are permitted before a consequence must be issued? What is the group's policy regarding tardiness?
- Decide what the group can tolerate in terms of attendance and participation and design consequences to be met if those guidelines are not met.
- Each group must have one research meeting outside of class. When and where will your group meet?
- Papers must be written in one voice. It may be useful to have a group "secretary" to keep notes of the discussion. Will this be a rotating job or will one person take the job for the length of the project?
- Begin to divide labor. Is one person strong at research and yet uncomfortable at public speaking? Discuss the strengths and weaknesses of the group members and divide the labor according to each member's ability.
- Do not be afraid to disagree. Your research will show you that the "experts" do not always agree. Bring this disagreement into your presentation and use it to negotiate your final understanding of the text. What are acceptable ways of voicing disagreement in your group what are acceptable means of reaching a consensus or an agreement to disagree?
- Do not disrespect your colleagues. Criticism and critique are tricky writing forms; you will learn how to disagree with someone in this class or in your research without being negative, slanderous or dismissive. This classroom cannot tolerate disrespect on any level. List one guideline that will help your group to avoid inadvertent disrespect. What is each member's idea of a disrespectful comment?
- Discuss and decide the level of grade toward which the group is working. Is everyone working toward an "A"? Is a "C" adequate for the majority of the group? Coordinate the level of energy each member is willing to put into the project.

HANDOUT

THIS HANDOUT WORKS WITH THE MULTICULTURAL READING PARADIGM HANDOUT AND THE QUESTIONS FROM THE END OF THE FAN SHEN ESSAY

The traditional reading model asks:
(Taken from Shen, 494)
      1. Why does Fan Shen say English composition is a cultural and social activity?
      2. What are the differences between Western and Chinese views of the self, according to Shen?
      3. What does Shen mean by the "Yijing" approach to writing?
      4. In a paragraph, summarize the process by which Fan Shen learned to write English composition essays.

The class interpreted these questions as follows:
      1. What is the author's main point?
      2. What is the larger cultural significance of the main point?
      3. How does the author illustrate the main point?
      4. What did the author say to support the main point?

The multicultural reading paradigm was interpreted as follows:
      1. How do you feel about what the author wrote?
      2. Why do you feel that way?
      3. Does the text help you to understand your own historical moment any differently than you previously understood it? How?
      4. Do you understand the world that produced the text any differently? How and why?

SYLLABUS
MULTICULTURAL READING

Required Texts:

China Men by Maxine Hong Kingston
M. Butterfly by David Henry Hwang

Graded Assignments:

    Two (2)-page response papers = 10%
    Seven (7) one-page review papers = 15%
    One (1) collaborative eight to ten-page final paper with rough draft = 20%
    One (1) collaborative class presentation = 20%
    Final Exam = 35%

Attendance and class participation will factor in for 10% of your final grade, but be aware that many of your graded assignments cannot be completed without your presence and participation in the work of the class.

Week One:
Monday 4/3: Introduction, in-class writing
Assignment: Read hand out: "The Classroom and the Wider Culture" by Fan Shen. BE PREPARED FOR CLASS DISCUSSION
Wednesday 4/5: CLASS DISCUSSION
Assignment: Read hand out: "multicultural reading paradigm" BE PREPARED FOR CLASS DISCUSSION
Friday 4/7: CLASS DISCUSSION
Assignment: 2 page (500 word) essay that responds to the Shen essay using the multicultural format. DUE ON MONDAY.

Week Two:
Monday 4/10: FIRST WRITING ASSIGNMENT DUE. BRING *CHINA MEN* and *M. BUTTERFLY* TO CLASS. We will organize discussion groups, assign chapters, and discuss format.

Wednesday 4/12: CLASS DISCUSSION—guidelines for collaborative group work
Assignment: Add two suggestions to the guidelines that I have provided. Think about practical suggestions that may help us to avoid problems in collaborative work. DUE IN CLASS ON FRIDAY.
Friday 4/14: CLASS DISCUSSION—collaborative work.
Assignment: Write a 2-page (500-word) essay that responds to the idea of collaborative writing, which we have been discussing in class this week. How do you feel about turning in a final paper that you have had to write with two other people—remember this will be a graded assignment that will count heavily towards your final grade. I expect an argument—not a reaction. Also, read "On Discovery," p. 3, and "On Fathers," p.6, in *China Men*. BE PREPARED FOR CLASS DISCUSSION

Week Three:
Monday 4/17: FIRST GRADED ASSIGNMENT DUE. Lesliee's class presentation of "On Discovery" and "On Fathers."
Assignment: One-page (250-word) review of Lesliee's class presentation. Lesliee will write a self-critique.
Wednesday 4/19: LIBRARY TOUR
Assignment: GROUP ONE PREPARE A FIVE-PAGE ROUGH DRAFT OF YOUR CLASS PRESENTATION BRING IT TO CLASS.
Friday 4/21: CLASS DISCUSSION—review of Lesliee's class presentation and self-critique, and workshop time for collaborative rough drafts
Assignment: Read *M. Butterfly*.

Week Four: Group One In Charge
Monday 4/24: GROUP ONE'S CLASS PRESENTATION
Assignment: Write a one-page (250-word) review of Group One's class presentation. Group One will write a collaborative self-critique on Friday.
Wednesday 4/26: CLASS DISCUSSION
Assignment: GROUP TWO PREPARE FIVE-PAGE ROUGH DRAFT. BRING IT TO CLASS.
Friday 4/28: COLLABORATIVE ROUGH DRAFT WORKSHOP
Assignment: Read "The Father from China" section of *China Men*. Pp. 9-74.

Week Five: Group: Two In Charge
Monday 5/1: GROUP TWO'S CLASS PRESENTATION
Assignment: Write a one-page (250-word) review of Group Two's class presentation. Group Two will write a collaborative self-critique on Friday.
Wednesday 5/3: CLASS DISCUSSION
Assignment: GROUP THREE PREPARE A FIVE-PAGE ROUGH DRAFT AND BRING IT TO CLASS.
Friday 5/5: COLLABORATIVE ROUGH DRAFT WORKSHOP
Assignment: Read "The Great Grandfather of the Sandalwood Mountains" section of *China Men*. Pp. 83-122.

Week Six: Group Three In Charge
Monday 5/8: GROUP THREE'S CLASS PRESENTATION
Assignment: Write a one-page (250-word) review of Group Three's class presentation. Group Three will write a collaborative self-critique on Friday.
Wednesday 5/10: CLASS DISCUSSION
Assignment: GROUP FOUR PREPARE A FIVE-PAGE ROUGH DRAFT AND BRING IT TO CLASS.
Friday 5/12: COLLABORATIVE ROUGH DRAFT WORKSHOP
Assignment: Read "The Grandfather of the Sierra Nevada Mountains" section in *China Men*. Pp. 123-160.

Week Seven: Group Four In Charge
Monday 5/15: GROUP FOUR'S CLASS PRESENTATION
Assignment: Write a one-page (250-word) review of Group Four's presentation. Group Four will write a collaborative self-critique on Friday.
Wednesday 5/17: CLASS DISCUSSION
Assignment: GROUP FIVE PREPARE A FIVE-PAGE ROUGH DRAFT AND BRING IT TO CLASS.
Friday 5/19: COLLABORATIVE ROUGH DRAFT WORKSHOP
Assignment: Read "The Making of More Americans" section of *China Men*. Pp. 163-224.

Week Eight: Group Five In Charge

Monday 5/22: GROUP FIVE'S CLASS PRESENTATION
Assignment: Write a one-page (250-word) review of Group Five's class presentation. Group Five will write a collaborative self-critique on Friday.
Wednesday 5/24: CLASS DISCUSSION
Assignment: GROUP SIX PREPARE A FIVE PAGE ROUGH DRAFT AND BRING IT TO CLASS.
Friday 5/26: COLLABORATIVE ROUGH DRAFT WORKSHOP
Assignment: Read "The American Father" section of *China Men*. Pp. 235-256.

ENJOY YOUR HOLIDAY

Week Nine: Group Six In Charge

Monday 5/29: HOLIDAY
Wednesday 5/31: GROUP SIX'S CLASS PRESENTATION
Assignment: Write a one page (250 word) review of Group Six's class presentation. Group Six will write a collaborative self-critique on Friday.
Friday 6/2: COLLABORATIVE ROUGH DRAFT WORKSHOP - at this point all groups will be working on rough drafts of their final paper.
Assignment: Read "The Brother in Vietnam" section in *China Men*. Pp. 261-307.

Week Ten: Lesliee Finishes *China Men*

Monday 6/5: LESLIEE'S CLASS PRESENTATION
Assignment: Write a one-page (250-word) review of Lesliee's final presentation.
Wednesday 6/7: Class discussion and final paper negotiation and workshop. The final paper is due on the day of the final.
Friday 6/9: Class discussion and review.

FINAL EXAM

Please write a minimum of one page in response to all three of the following questions:

1 What is multiculturalism? Consider the ways in which your understanding of this term may or may not have changed over the course of the quarter.

2. How was traditional grading (the teacher gives the grades) a problem in the context of our non-traditional classroom? Do you have any suggestions for a more democratic form of grading or do you think grades should only be given by the teacher? As part of this question please tell me what you see as the traditional role of the teacher in a college classroom and how Lesliee did or did not follow this model.

3. Discuss the positive and negative aspects of collaborative work. This is your chance to tell me who did or did not fully participate in ways that were satisfactory to the group. However, I would really like for you to focus on the process. Tell me about the conversations you had in trying to hash out topics for presentation and papers.

Bibliography

Althusser, Louis. "Ideological and Ideological State Apparatuses (Notes Towards an Investigation) (January-April 1969)." In *Lenin and Philosophy: and Other Essays by Louis Althusser*. New York: Monthly Review Press, 1971.

Appiah, K. Anthony. "The Multicultural Misunderstanding." *New York Review of Books* (October 9, 1997): 30-36.

Appleton, Nicholas. *Multiculturalism and the Courts*. Los Angeles: National Dissemination and Assessment Center, 1978.

Auerbach, Susan, ed. *Encyclopedia of Multiculturalism,* Volume 1. New York: Marshall Cavendish, 1994.

Bak, Hans, ed. *Multiculturalism and the Canon of American Culture*. Amsterdam: Vu University Press, 1993.

Baker, Houston A. "To Move without Moving: An Analysis of Creativity and Commerce in Ralph Ellison's Trueblood Episode." *Speaking for You: The Vision of Ralph Ellison*. Washington, DC: Howard University Press, 1987.

Bartholomae, Donald. "Inventing the University." *When a Writer Can't Write: Studies in Writer's Block and Other Composing-Process Problems*. Mike Rose, ed. New York: Guilford Press, 1985.

Bellah, Robert. *Habits of the Heart: Individualism and Commitment in American Life*. Berkeley: University of California Press, 1985.

Bentson, Kimberly W. "Introduction." *Speaking for You: The Vision of Ralph Ellison*. Washington, DC: Howard University Press, 1987.

Bernstein, Richard. *Dictatorship of Virtue: Multiculturalism and the Battle for America's Future*. New York: Alfred A. Knopf, 1994.

Bhabha, Homi K. *The Location of Culture*. New York: Routledge, 1994.

Bizjak, Tony. "U.S. Gets Prod to See Colors in Broad Range." *The Press-Enterprise* (October 4, 1994): A1-A7.

Bizzell, Patricia. *Academic Discourse and Critical Consciousness*. Pittsburgh, Pennsylvania: University of Pittsburgh Press, 1992.

Bloom, Allan. *The Closing of the American Mind*. New York: Simon and Schuster, 1987.

Brodkey, Linda. "On the Subjects of Class and Gender in 'The Literacy of Letters.'" *College English* 51(2) (February 1989): 125-141.

Brown, Dee. *Bury My Heart at Wounded Knee: An Indian History of the American West*. New York: Henry Holt and Company, 1970.

Buenker, John D. and Lorman A. Ratner, eds. *Multiculturalism in the United States: A Comparative Guide to Acculturation and Ethnicity*. New York: Greenwood Press, 1992.

Butler, Judith. *Gender Trouble: Feminism and the Subversion of Identity*. New York: Routledge, 1990.

Cheney, Lynne. *Humanities in America: A Report to the President, the Congress, and the American People*. National Endowment of the Humanities, 1988.

Chicago Cultural Studies Group. "Critical Multiculturalism." *Critical Inquiry* 18(3) (spring 1992): 530-555.

Coiner, Constance. "Is Multiculturalism Enough?" *Women's Studies* 20(3-4) (1992): 209-215.

Cruse, Harold. *The Crisis of the Negro Intellectual*. New York: William Morrow & Co., Inc., 1967.

D'Souza, Dinesh. *Illiberal Education: The Politics of Race and Sex on Campus*. New York: Free Press, 1991.

Dyer, Richard. "White." *Screen* 29(4) (1988): 44-64.

Edmundson, Mark. "On the Uses of a Liberal Education: As Lite Entertainment for Bored College Students." *Harper's* (September 1997): 39-49.

Edwards, Ronald G. "Multiculturalism and Its Links to Quality Education and Democracy." *Multicultural Review* 2(2) (June 1993): 12-16, 19.

Ellison, Ralph. *Invisible Man*. New York: Random House, Vintage Books, 1989.

Erickson, Peter. "Multiculturalism and the Problem of Liberalism." *Reconstruction* 2(1) (1992): 97-101.

Fisher Fishkin, Shelly. *Was Huck Black? Mark Twain and African American Voices*. New York: Oxford University Press, 1993.

Ford, Nick Aaron. *Black Studies: Threat or Challenge*. Port Washington, New York: National University Publications, 1973.

Forgacs, David and Geoffrey Nowell-Smith, eds. *Antonio Gramsci: Selections from Cultural Writings*. Cambridge: Harvard University Press, 1985.

Foucault, Michel. "The Great Confinement" from *Madness and Civilization.* In *The Foucault Reader.* New York: Pantheon Books, 1984a.
— — —. "Space, Knowledge and Power." In *The Foucault Reader.* New York: Pantheon Books, 1984b.
Friere, Paolo. *Education for Critical Consciousness.* New York: Seabury, 1973.
— — —. "Letter to North-American Teachers." In *Friere For the Classroom: A Sourcebook for Liberatory Teaching.* Ira Shor, ed. Portsmouth, New Hampshire: Boynton/Cook Publishers, 1987.
— — —. *Pedagogy of the Oppressed.* New York: Continuum, 1993.
Gates, Henry Louis, Jr. *"Race," Writing and Difference.* Chicago: University of Chicago Press, 1985.
— — —. *The Signifying Monkey: A Theory of Afro American Literary Criticism.* New York: Oxford University Press, 1988.
— — —. "Good-bye Columbus? Notes on the Culture of Criticism." *American Literary History* 3(4) (winter 1991): 711-727.
— — —. "Beyond the Culture Wars: Identities in Dialogue." *Profession 93.* New York: Modern Language Association, 1993: 6-11.
Gates, Henry Louis, Jr., ed. *Classic Slave Narratives.* New York: Penguin Books, 1987.
Geok-Lin Lim, Shirley. *Approaches to Teaching Kingston's "The Woman Warrior."* New York: Modern Language Association of America, 1991.
Geyer, Michael. "Multiculturalism and the Politics of General Education." *Critical Inquiry* 19(3) (spring 1993): 499-533.
Giroux, Henry. *Schooling and the Struggle for Public Life.* Minneapolis: University of Minnesota Press, 1988.
— — —. *Theory and Resistance in Education: A Pedagogy for the Opposition. Critical Perspectives in Social Theory Series.* New York: Bergin & Garvey, 1983.
— — —. "Cultural Studies, Resisting Difference, and the Return of Critical Pedagogy." In *Border Crossings: Cultural Workers and the Politics of Education.* New York: Routledge, 1992.
— — —. *Living Dangerously: Multiculturalism and the Politics of Difference.* New York: Peter Lang, 1993.

———. "Living Dangerously: Identity Politics and the New Cultural Racism." In *Between Borders: Pedagogy and the Politics of Cultural Studies*. Henry Giroux and Peter McLaren, eds. New York: Routledge, 1994.

Goddu, Teresa A. and Craig V. Smith. "Scenes of Writing in Frederick Douglass's Narrative: Autobiography and the Creation of Self." *The Southern Review* 25(4) (autumn, 1989): 822.

Goldberg, David Theo. "The Social Formation of Racist Discourse." *Anatomy of Racism*. David Theo Goldberg, ed. Minneapolis, Minnesota: Minnesota University Press, 1990.

Gunew, Sneja and Kateryna O. Longley, eds. *Striking Chords: Multicultural Literary Interpretations*. Sydney Australia: Allen and Unwin, 1992.

Habermas, Jurgen. "Theory and Practice." *Theory and Practice*. Boston: Beacon Press, 1973.

Henderson, Algo D. and Jean Glidden Henderson. *Higher Education in America: Problems, Priorities and Prospects*. San Francisco: Jossey-Bass, 1974.

Hirsch, E. D. *Cultural Literacy: What Every American Needs to Know*. Boston: Houghton Mifflin, 1987.

hooks, bell. *Yearnings*. Boston: South End Press, 1990.

———. "Representations of Whiteness in the Black Imagination." *Black Looks: Race and Representation*. Boston: South End Press, 1992: 165-178.

Horton, John, ed. *Liberalism, Multiculturalism and Toleration*. New York: St. Martin's Press, 1993.

Hwang, David Henry. *M Butterfly*. New York: Penguin Books, 1989.

Jackson, Margaret Y. *Slave Narratives of the Pre-Civil War Period: 1840-1860*. Chicago: Adams Press, 1976.

Jefferson, Thomas. "Report of the Commissioners for the University of Virginia." In *The Portable Jefferson*. Merrill D. Peterson, ed. New York: Penguin, 1977.

Kanpol, Barry and Peter McLaren. *Critical Multiculturalism*. Westport, Connecticut: Greenwood Press, 1995

Keating, AnnLouise. "Interrogating 'Whiteness,' (De)Constructing 'Race.'" *College English* 57(8) (December 1995): 901-918.

Kingston, Maxine Hong. *The Woman Warrior: Memoirs of A Childhood Among Ghosts*. New York: Random House, Vintage Books, 1977.

———. *China Men*. New York: Random House, Vintage Books, 1989.

Kitzhaber, Albert. *Rhetoric in American Colleges: 1850-1900*. Dallas: Southern Methodist University Press, 1990.

Kuhn, Thomas. *The Structure of Scientific Revolutions*. Chicago: University of Chicago Press, 1970.

Lauter, Paul. *Canons and Contexts*. Oxford: Oxford University Press, 1991.

Lester, Julius. "Morality and *Adventures of Huckleberry Finn*." In *Mark Twain, Adventures of Huckleberry Finn: A Case Study in Critical Controversy*. Gerald Graff and James Phelan, eds. Boston: Bedford, 1995.

Levin, Kim, ed. *Beyond Wall and Wars: Art, Politics, and Multiculturalism*. New York: Midmarch Arts Press, 1992.

Lipset, Seymour Martin and Sheldon S. Wolin, eds. *The Berkeley Student Revolt: Facts and Interpretations*. New York: Doubleday, 1965.

Lu, Min-Zhan. "Professing Multiculturalism: The Politics of Style in the Contact Zone." *College Composition and Communication* 45(4) (December 1994): 442-458.

Ludwig, Saemi. *Concrete Language: Intercultural Communication in Maxine Hong Kingston's "The Woman Warrior: Memoirs of a Girlhood Among Ghosts" and Ishmael Reed's "Mumbo Jumbo."* Frankfurt am Main, Bern, New York: Peter Lang, 1996.

Lye, Colleen. "*M. Butterfly* and the Rhetoric of Anti-essentialism." In *The Ethnic Canon*. David Palumbo-Liu, ed. Minneapolis: University of Minnesota Press, 1995.

Maasik, Sonia and J. Solomon, eds. *Signs of Life in the U.S.A.: Readings on Popular Culture for Writers*. Boston: Bedford Books of St. Martin's Press, 1994.

Madison, James. "Federalist Paper Number 63, March 1, 1788." In *The Federalist Papers*. Gary Wills, ed. New York: Bantam Books, 1982.

Marx, Leo. "Mr. Eliot, Mr. Trilling and *Huckleberry Finn*." In *Mark Twain, Adventures of Huckleberry Finn: A Case Study in Critical Controversy*. Gerald Graff and James Phelan, eds. Boston: Bedford, 1995.

Matsuda, Mari, J., C. R. Lawrence, III, R. Delgado, and K.W. Crenshaw. *Words that Wound: Critical Race Theory, Assaultive Speech, and The First Amendment*. Boulder, Colorado: Westview Press, 1993.

McCormick, Kathleen. *The Culture of Reading and the Teaching of English*. Manchester, Eng.: Manchester University Press, 1994.

Miller, Susan. *Textual Carnivals: The Politics of Composition*. Carbondale, IL: Southern Illinois University Press, 1991.

Moraga, Cherríe and Gloria Anzaldúa, eds. *This Bridge Called My Back: Writings by Racial Women of Color*. New York: Kitchen Table Women of Color Press, 1981.

Morrison, Toni. *Playing in the Dark: Whiteness and the Literary Imagination*. Cambridge, MA: Harvard University Press, 1992.

Nelson, Cary. "Canon Fodder: An Evening with William Bennett, Lynne Cheney, and Dinesh D'Souza." *Works and Days: Essays in the Socio-Historical Dimensions of Literature and the Arts* 18 (fall 1991): 39-54.

Nishime, LeiLani. "Engendering Genre: Gender and Nationalism in *China Men* and *The Woman Warrior.*" *MELUS* 20(1) (spring 1995): 76-82.

Ostendorf, Berndt. "PC, or Do the Right Thing." In *Multiculturalism and the Canon of American Culture*. Hans Bak, ed. Amsterdam: Vu University Press, 1993.

Palumbo-Liu, David, ed. *The Ethnic Canon*. Minneapolis: University of Minnesota Press, 1995.

Ping, Tang Soo. "Ralph Ellison and K. S. Maniam: Ethnicity in America and Malaysia, Two Kinds of Invisibility," *MELUS* 18(4) (winter 1993-1994): 81-97.

Quinn, Ed and Leonard Kriegel. "Open Admissions Revisited: How the Dream Was Deferred." *The Nation* 238(13) (April 7, 1984): 412-414.

Ravitch, Diane. "Multiculturalism: E Pluribus Plures." *American Scholar* 59(3) (summer, 1990): 337.

Rizvi Fazal. *Ethnicity, Class and Multicultural Education*. Victoria, Canada: Deakin University Press, 1986.

Rodriguez, Clara. *Puerto Ricans: Born in the U. S. A.* Boulder, Colorado: Westview Press, 1991.

Rowlandson, Mary. "The Narrative of the Captivity and Restoration of Mrs. Mary Rowlandson." In *Original Narratives of Early American History, Narratives of Indian Wars 1675-1699 XIV*. C. H. Lincoln, ed. New York: Barnes and Noble, 1952.

Shen, Fan. "The Classroom and the Wider Culture: Identity as a Key to Learning English Composition." In *Signs of Life in the USA: Readings on Popular Culture for Writers*. Sonia Maasik and J. Solomon, eds. Boston: Bedford Books of St. Martin's Press, 1994.

Shor, Ira. *Friere for the Classroom: A Sourcebook for Liberatory Teaching*. Portsmouth, NH: Boynton/Cook Publishers, 1987.

— — —. *Empowering Education: Critical Teaching for Social Change*. Chicago: The University of Chicago Press, 1992.

Shor, Ira and Paolo Friere. *A Pedagogy for Liberation: Dialogues on Transforming Education.* South Hadley, MA: Bergin & Garvey, 1987.

Simonson, Rick and Scott Walker, eds. *The Graywolf Annual Five: Multicultural Literacy.* St. Paul: Graywolf Press, 1988.

Sklar, Holly. *Chaos or Community: Seeking Solutions, Not Scapegoats for Bad Economics.* Boston: South End Press, 1995.

Smith, David L. "Huck, Jim and American Racial Discourse." In *Satire Or Evasion: Black Perspectives on Huckleberry Finn.* James S. Leonard, Thomas A. Tenney, and Thadious M. Davis, eds. Durham, NC: Duke University Press, 1992.

Spiller, Hortense. "Ellison's 'Usable Past': Toward a Theory of Myth." *Speaking for You: The Vision of Ralph Ellison.* Washington, DC: Howard University Press, 1987.

Suleri, Sara. "Multiculturalism and Its Discontents." *Profession 93*, New York: Modern Language Association (1993): 16-17.

Sundquist, Eric J. *To Wake the Nations: Race in the Making of American Literature.* Cambridge, MA: Harvard University Press, 1993.

Takaki, Ronald. *A Different Mirror: A History of Multicultural America.* New York: Little, Brown and Company, 1993.

Trueba, Henry. "Race and Ethnicity: The Role of Universities in Healing Multicultural America." *Educational Theory* 43(1) (winter 1993): 41-54.

Twain, Mark. *Adventures of Huckleberry Finn.* In *Mark Twain, Adventures of Huckleberry Finn: A Case Study in Critical Controversy.* Gerald Graff and James Phelan, eds. Boston: Bedford, 1995.

Wallerstein, Immanuel and Paul Starr, eds. *The University Crisis Reader, I, II.* New York: Random House 1971.

Whitaker, Thomas R. "Spokesman for Invisibility." *Speaking for You: The Vision of Ralph Ellison.* Washington, DC: Howard University Press, 1987.

Wolf, Bryan. "Firing the Canon." *American Literary History* 3(4) (winter 1991): 707-710.

Worsham, Lynn. "Writing against Writing: The Predicament of Écriture Feminine in Composition Studies." In *Contending With Words.* Patricia Harkin and John Schilb, eds. New York: Modern Language Association, 1991.

Wright, Richard. "The Man Who Lived Underground." In *Eight Men.* New York: World Publishing, 1961.

Yamada, Mitsuye and Sarie Sachie Hylkema, eds. *Sowing Ti Leaves: Writings by Multicultural Women.* Irvine, California: Multicultural Women Writers of Orange County, 1990.

Young, R. *White Mythologies: Writing History and the West.* New York: Routledge, 1990.

Index

Accommodation, 22, 26, 28, 31, 33, 35, 47, 52, 80, 116 n. 2
Adventures of Huckleberry Finn, 70, 79, 87
    Huck Finn, 70, 71, 79, 81, 87
        as narrator of the escape, 75
        as privileged author, 72
    Jim, 70-79, 87
        as the prisoner, 77
    Tom, 70-78, 81, 87
        as critic and gatekeeper, 73
Affirmative action, 39, 65 n. 6
African American, 26, 28, 77, 80, 89 n. 9, 111
Afrocentrism, 32, 33
Agency, 58, 66 n. 11, 71, 74, 76, 86, 108
American
  academy, 13, 27, 30
  canon, 14
  character, 19, 31
  culture, 13-20, 22-24, 26, 28, 30-33, 36 n. 2, 37 n. 11, 43, 60-63, 65 n. 1, 68, 79, 88 n. 1, 113, 115, 116 n. 6
  identity, 17, 23, 25, 26, 28, 31, 33, 67
  multiculturalism, 16, 96
  university, 15, 16, 18, 19, 20, 26, 28, 36 n. 5
Anglo-American, 35, 112
Appearance, 18, 19, 22, 27, 41, 44
Appleton, Nicholas, 14, 22
Asian American, 26, 28
Assimilation, 16, 17, 22, 24, 36 n. 3, 44, 47, 71, 74, 76, 78, 100, 113

Battle Royale, 81
Bhabha, Homi K., 47, 48
Bloom, Allan, 14, 32, 37 n. 7
Brodkey, Linda, 51-54

Cable, George Washington, 84, 90 n. 11
Cheney, Lynne, 32, 34, 54
Chicano/a, 24-26, 33
Civil Rights Movement, 25, 27
Class presentation, 102, 109
Committee of Ten, 20
Constitution, the, 17
Critical literacy, 115
Critical multicultural pedagogy, 93-95, 97, 99, 114, 115
Critical multicultural reading paradigm, 116 n. 3, 117 n. 7
Critical theory, 40, 115
Culture wars, 20

Demons, 86, 87, 88, 90 n.16
Dialectic, 39, 48, 64
Difference, 15, 16, 22, 23, 25, 35, 39, 42, 68, 93-97, 99, 100, 105, 107, 112, 113, 115, 116 n. 5, 117 n. 8
  cultural, 14, 17, 28, 53, 57, 29, 77, 78
  economic, 44
  physical, 26
  physiognomic, 33, 54, 57
  physiological, 54, 78, 81, 83, 85, 88

Dominant culture, 18, 20, 22, 23, 27, 28, 31, 32, 34, 36, 37 n. 11 43, 46, 50, 57, 63, 68, 69, 71, 78, 79, 82, 83, 84, 86, 99, 115

Education
 banking, 95, 96
 citizenship, 40, 41, 94, 104
 higher, 19, 20, 26, 27, 94, 97
 liberatory, 94, 106
 problem-posing, 94, 104, 110, 114
Ellison, Ralph, 68, 76, 79, 81-83, 84
 Invisible Man, 68, 76, 79, 81-83, 85, 89n. 9
Encyclopedia of Multiculturalism, 13

Feminist theory, 49, 89, n. 2
Fisher Fishkin, Shelley, 73, 74, 89 n. 3
Foucault, Michel, 106, 112
Frankfurt School, the, 40
Friere, Paolo, 40, 95-100, 104, 115

Gates, Henry Louis, Jr., 14, 33 57, 58, 59, 89 n. 5, 90 n. 14
Generative themes, 95, 100, 101, 116 n. 5
Ghosts, 85-87
Giroux, Henry, 38 n. 13, 40, 41, 46, 54-57, 61, 64 n. 1, 94, 97, 99, 104, 115
Globalism, 16, 94, 96
Goldberg, David Theo, 59, 60, 61, 62, 63, 64
Gramsci, Antonio, 14, 15, 24

Habermas, Jurgen, 50, 52, 54
Hegemony, 14, 15, 24, 79, 81

Hong Kingston, Maxine
 China Men, 68, 85, 87, 88 90 n. 16, 112
 The Woman Warrior: A Memoir of a Childhood Spent Among Ghosts, 68, 85-88

hooks, bell, 54, 55, 58, 59, 67, 80, 81-83, 87

Identity, 46, 47, 66 n. 11
 fixed, 69, 98
 social/cultural, 14, 57, 65 n. 7, 106
Ideology, 61, 65 n. 2, 108, 112
Interruption, 52, 53

Jefferson, Thomas, 18, 19
 1818 Report to the Commissioners for the University of Virginia, 18

Kanpol, Barry, 64 n. 1
Keating, AnnLouise, 45, 46, 67

Liberal/Conservative tension, 16, 17, 19, 29, 32, 34, 35, 52, 56
Liberty, 106, 111, 114
Lim, Shirley Geok-Lin, 90 n.12
Literary tradition, 70, 77, 79
Logic of domination, the, 61
Lu, Min-Zhan, 14, 50, 51

Madison, James, 17-20, 41
 Federalist Paper No. 63, 18
McCormick, Kathleen, 99, 107, 108, 109
McLaren, Peter, 64 n. 1
Miller, Susan
 Textual Carnivals: The Politics of Composition, 22
Monocultural, 14, 17, 18, 22, 23, 29, 31, 35, 47, 115
Morrison, Toni, 67, 70, 71, 75, 78, 79, 84, 85

Multicultural demographics, 13, 20, 39

Native American, 25, 26, 28, 33
Nishime, LeiLani, 88, 91 n. 18

Pluralism, 14, 23, 26
Power, 15, 39, 41, 45, 46, 52, 56,

61, 67-70, 72, 74, 76-88, 96, 97,
    99, 100, 105-108, 110-114
Proposition 187, 110

Race, 15, 34, 35, 43-47, 54-60, 61-
    63, 86, 86, 98
  racial, 13, 26, 42-46, 49, 53-57,
      59, 60, 63, 87, 97, 100
  racism, 43, 52, 55, 59, 61, 83,
      108
  racist, 43, 44, 54, 57-63, 69
Racialization of poverty, 42, 59
Radical theory, 46, 51, 56
Ravitch, Diane, 14, 37
Remediation, 23, 29, 30, 32
Representation, 14, 18-20, 22, 26,
    30, 33, 35, 36, 43, 45, 49, 51, 52,
    54, 58, 69, 74, 80,   85, 97, 115,
    116
Rodriguez, Clara, 44

Senate, the, 18, 19
Shor, Ira, 40, 52, 94, 98, 99, 100,
    109, 116
Spivak, Gayatri, 60, 61
Subject, 60, 86, 88, 96
  black, 25, 26, 33, 42, 55, 57, 58,
      78, 80, 82-84, 89-91
  human, 88
  red, 78
  unified American, 47, 51
  white, 42-49, 55-58, 60, 63, 67,
      70, 71, 76, 78, 79, 80-84,
      86, 106, 113
  yellow, 78
Subject of discourse, 23, 73, 99
Subjectivity(ies), 40, 47, 49, 52,
    55-57, 59, 60, 62, 65, 67, 75, 80,
    93, 97
Sundquist, Eric, 70
  *To Wake the Nations: Race in
      the Making of American
      Literature*, 90 n.11

Template of discourse, 73
Trope of visibility, 39, 43, 45, 56,
    67-69, 76, 77, 81-87, 89 n. 9
Trueba, Henry, 65 n. 1
Twain, Mark, 68, 69, 70, 71, 72,
    74, 76, 77, 78, 80, 87

Universities
  City University of New York
      (CUNY), 26, 27, 29, 31
  Harvard, 20, 21, 22, 27, 29
  University of California,
      Berkeley, 24, 25, 26, 28,
      29, 30, 31, 33

Western European Tradition, 19,
    28, 74
Women's Rights Movement, 27

About the Author

LESLIEE ANTONETTE is Assistant Professor of English, East Stroudsburg University, Pennsylvania.

ISBN 0-89789-546-0

90000>

EAN

9 780897 895460

HARDCOVER BAR CODE